ATÉ MÁS

Latinx Futurisms

ATÉ MAIS

Latinx Futurisms

Edited by

Alan Chazaro
Malcolm Friend
Kim Sousa

Deep Vellum Publishing
3000 Commerce Street, Dallas, Texas 75226
deepvellum.org · @deepvellum

Deep Vellum is a 501c3 nonprofit literary arts organization founded in 2013 with the mission to bring the world into conversation through literature.

FIRST EDITION, 2024

Support for this publication has been provided in part by grants from the National Endowment for the Arts, the Texas Commission on the Arts, the City of Dallas Office of Arts and Culture, the Communities Foundation of Texas, Anaphora Literary Arts, and the Addy Foundation.

LIBRARY OF CONGRESS CATALOGING-IN-PUBLICATION DATA

LCCN: 2024020397

Cover art and design byVictoria Peña
Interior layout and typesetting by David Wojciechowski

PRINTED IN CANADA

To those who have come before us,
those who are here with us,
and those who will come after us—
see you in the stars.

TABLE OF CONTENTS

ATÉ MAIS

Latinx Futurisms

EDITOR'S NOTE

Dear comrade,

In Brazil, we say "até mais" when we're leaving friends. In conceptualizing an anthology of Latinx Futurisms as a space we want to hold for our community—our friends—we wanted to lean on both the common usage of the phrase—"until I see you again"—and the literal translation—"until more."

This anthology is the hope for both: until we see each other again in the future, and until we see each other again in a future that holds more possibilities for us. This is an anti-colonial future, an anti-capitalist future, a borderless, abolitionist future. It's important to us that this future also challenges "Latinx" as an identifier: we resist the too-often whitewashed displays of the "Latinidad." It's essential to our future to imagine a more equitable and representative community—one where our Black, Indigenous, and Queer siblings are at the table breaking future bread with us. Coming from Brazil, I know firsthand that white Latinxs are not the face of my country, one people so often like to say is "faceless." In *Até Mais*, we're challenging that dangerous flattening and conflation of our varied experiences: What could be "faceless" about us? Together, we can define ourselves beyond the colonialist projects set against our ancestors by rejecting branqueamento/blanqueamiento, machismo, and anti-Indigenous settler culture.

Instead, all of us dreamers here hold a mirror to our collective dreamland: our complete world, our every face and freedom. We play Solange's "A Seat at the Table" and feast.

I'm honored to curate this project with my co-editors, Malcolm Friend and Alan Chazaro—the two forward-reaching poets who inspired this anthology. Malcolm with his poem "Portrait of the Author in Plátano Heaven" and Alan with his manuscript of "Pocho Boy" Futurisms. Together, we are three poets representing the diaspora from North and South America (Mexico, Brazil) and the Caribbean (Puerto Rico). We are Black, Brown, and Mixed. We are immigrants and first- and second-generation

Americans. Nineties kids to the end, we see this anthology as a project For Us By Us—through every expression of "Us."

If we are seeds, let us be heirloom: always evolving and unbound.

Até Mais, queridxs—we'll see you on the other side.

In community, in arms, and in gratitude,

Kim Sousa

Malcolm Friend

POLYNEGRO THEORY

Soon, the country will look more like us,
mixed race folk keep saying, and I know
they mean ambiguous. I think of my mom:
woman, skin the tone of earth.
When me and my siblings were kids,
strangers would ask her, *Are they yours?*
and, *What are they mixed with?*
Always the doubt that we could ever be kin.
Always the fascination, trying to place us
as something other than Black.
I think of all the times I have been denied
anything other than Blackness.
The cops who rushed me in Seattle
on my way out Safeway. The cop in Spain
who stopped me on my way out the train station.
Mom, who hated when people referred to us as mixed,
never referred to us as anything but Black.
Our ambiguous dad, who never once corrected her,
who knew how his children would walk through the world.
I think of my love, how she calls our hypothetical kids
polynegro: Puerto Rican, Jamaican, Malagasy, Black American.
And isn't that its own type of resistance?
Telling the Americas' post-racial voices
we will never imagine
a future without Blackness.

J. C. Rodriguez

IN THE FUTURE, I STOP SAYING HISPANIC

after José Olivarez

In the future, I go back home
& our kids who go to the "good schools"
don't have to self-flagellate anymore.
There are no zones; no districts; no lines
drawn in generational blood. Those kids stop
screaming "la migra" during hide & seek—
sacrifice is not a joke to make the white kids laugh.

In the future, our kids read more comic books;
find characters like them—lanterns & psions & outsiders
& heroes & lovers & survivors & there is nothing
exotic or dangerous about it.

In the future, I saved my hairline & still apply
Suavecito or Murray's every morning, committing
to my routine without digging pomade directly
into the scalp; without singing along to Morrissey.
We finally got rid of Morrissey.

I find the nerve to get Lady Guadalupe tattooed
over my whole back.

In the future, the good homie gets out of jail
—pero he's different.
We skate to Karina's Deli and he tells me
all about it over sancocho & Modelos.
I tell him his mom is doing okay; that his girl is waiting for him.
I squeeze the knives from his back

so when they hold him,
all they can feel is his softness.

In the future, I stop hiding
behind Latine or Latinx or Latino.
I call myself Peruvian—
know a little more about a family
that loved me. Hold my tías, set a prayer
for nana & find a way to say,
with all my gratitude:
you have always been a home.

Christopher "Rooster" Martinez

& IF NOT TOMORROW

this summer will still be a scorcher
—only softballs will not crack free
of their skins in sandlots

Nor

nightclubs drizzle sweat
where beer gulps us with its frost
& the girls dance themselves loose
of the forty-hour work week

Nor

jeune amour rifling through a throng
finding lips to kiss over Dua Lipa tracks
at kickbacks

Nor

handshakes & dap hugs
that solidify the bonds
that bind—a cherishment

Nor water parks theme parks
movie theater AC

the *you come to my side of town this week*
& I will go to your side, next week
the flatline lovers who
music & sway & sangria
& moonlight

No—we will wear our skins & wait

& yes

we will survive
another hot one to dance

(maybe tomorrow

& if not tomorrow
then maybe
tomorrow tomorrow)

& that day

will break open every hydrant

& the whole city will be Splashtown

& the city will be bodies evaporating

into the sun

sweating into night
domino hands reaching across tables
slapping down sunrise
crown & coke & ice fusing
like fond memories

& we will hold hands
like we remember

Vincent Toro

BLANCA CANALES VERSION 2.0

Arising from the slipstream
of obsolete memes and blurry
defunct html pages,
Blanca Canales is resurrected
as a firewall-smashing,
cyber-troll-annihilating digital phoenix.
A block of hacker coding designed
to stampede the freeloading
selfie vultures swooping into Camuy
and Fajardo cadging for tax breaks,
spreading their pestilence to millions
of innocent conches. Now, unbound
by biology, Blanca is free to live
as a C++ diasporic demigoddess,
melting hard drives, harboring drafts
of the PROMESA bill, rebooting CPUs
to vanquish TARP and the Monroe Doctrine.
Blanca 2.0 the Impaler marches
through mobile hotspots, embeds a bug
that changes all mention of the Rossellós
to read comemierdas.
She blasts all members of the junta
with radioactive signals
to give them a rare form of cancer,
heretofore known as "Cornelius Rhoads Disease."
Once she has organized
every crab and lizard into a militia,
she'll order them to pinch every gentrifier
and chase them off their vacation plots in Condado.
Only then will she retire to Jayuya

to play with our grandkids for all eternity,
or at least until the sun no longer
smooches with the palmas
on a queen-sized bed of blue sand.

Joel Salcido

ADELANTE TO THE INFINITE OUTWARD

—in cruise we move slow
ain't no hurry for the ranfla to levitate. our all-time highs made fuel. this machine equipped
w/ perpetual motion put some funkadelic in the tank & we fly. Teotihuacán
a parking lot, spaceships circling its crown like a halo.
out here, cucarachas selling chucherías in the floating fayuca, the María Sabina hologram
peddling tamales de hongos calientitos, & we came w/ hambre—
a hunger for everything denied in our past lives.

we land in a carnival
of Cantinflas clones performing
La Pocha Nostra, Guillermo Gómez-Peña on a Golden Eagle scowling
like a jaguar, his gray hair boundless as a Fibonacci spiral
braided into a ladder threaded through
the eye of the Sun Pyramid. we see llamas in the llanos of our murmurs,
stretch our fingers to the expanse of sun rays
we touch the heat but don't burn our hands
used to gripping realities hot as a comal.

There's a poetry workshop in Nahuatl. all the BROWNS
wonder-laboring to conjure a new word for bigote, training Xolos
for a trip to Mictlán
to find Octavio Paz & get the chisme
on the unpublished conjugations of chingar.
every alleyway sings a mariachi of oyes y quihúboles,
Chicano power handshakes rattle
to the fault lines, chancla dodging Olympics are held in the ancient ball courts
officiated by María Félix tronando her chicharrones through a loudspeaker.
here, we all BROWN buffalos, all phantasmagoric mariposas, impervious Axolotl

—but we don't need to roam or cocoon or grow back our hearts.

all the velas stay lit not to mourn but to light the landing strips—
everywhere a landing strip pulling up in stretch Astro(cara)vans,
swivel chairs rotating along the orbit of the Mayan codex.
we fix our mascara in the gold-rimmed mirrors,
our cat eyes growling lips lined into angel—alas our idle hands
embrujados weaving armor out of rosaries.

here we don't need armor. our skin has barked
all the stray dogs of Aztlán curled under our feet
so we don't need to touch ground.
our teeth are jaded fangs & chrome-grilled & weariless
our bones—hollowed & hallowed
uncut by steel volando y volado dreaming all our impossible
wings

Tatiana Figueroa Ramirez

AFTER THE REVOLUTION

Sunrises capture hues artists could never recreate.
Too vibrant for canvas to contain. The horizon
hugs oceans & clouds together where the highest peaks
of land kiss us all in greeting.

Alarm clocks are sonidos del campo or
Fania All-Stars or boleros para abuela.

I don't have to scavenge
for pasteles ingredients in the "Latin Food" aisle,
Megamart, or Bestway. Pan soba'o is not a dream
found only in tropical humidity.

A bridge connects la isla to the mainland
adorned with iridescent coral reefs & blessed
by waves, allowing safe passage to the children of Inés y Agüeybaná.

Rivers flow upstream & downstream quenching
the thirst of each mouth they touch.

Roots ripped from the mountains
& branches burned to the dirt
resurrected by agua florida.

Las fiestas patronales bring back Frankie, Hector, & Celia.
After fireworks, dance bomba with the stars & sea breezes
birthing rhythms only angels conjure.

Calderos on stoves molded by sofrito,
sazón, aceite, y ajo wake the warmth of Mami Tita
to ward off chills only the Northeast knows.

Books of de Burgos, García Márquez y Neruda mimic
the voice of Evelyn each time their spines bend
to retell stories a century old.

Houses do not crack
to an earthquake, twist
to a hurricane, or crumble
to whitetongued dollar signs.

Spanglish is declared
an official language. Dialects & slang
belong to no hierarchies paying homage
to a Spanish crown that forgot
our lands before we were ever born.

Where are you from?
is not a question.

Everyone understands
we were pillaged, deemed
unholy.

My father & brother, husband & son will never fight
in a war not theirs to welcome
a bullet carved with another man's name.

The people do not fear their own power, raising
a flag of their own design to chant their strength
across now-erased borders.

Even dogs, cats, & chickens with no homes
know they own the streets they roam.

The shackles of our great-great-grandfathers are made
into a crucifix, an altar, a sanctuary. We pray
for their forgiveness.

The cemetery stops being
the brightest place in el pueblo.

The church stops being
the center of el pueblo.

Despojos are not brujería.
Santería is not del diablo.
Catholicism is not the only way to heaven.

I am not looked at as an alien
& my hair is not questioned.
Nor my skin nor my accent nor my name.

I am not labeled foreigner by those unwilling to admit
Americans are born in more than one country.

& a coquí sits by my window each night, ensuring
my mother will never stop singing.

Tatiana Figueroa Ramirez

TO MY SON

I must tell you
this life will not be
easy for you. You born
into a cradle of thorns you will leave
my womb already scarred
by the fire set to burn you.
You who resemble
the warmth of the sunrise, competing
with the night sky. You carry
the light conjured & consumed
by the ancestors who dreamed
of your well-being. & somehow
you will only spark
Fear. Hate. & Rage
from those who don't understand you.
Those who have never been blessed
to witness such a gift as yourself.

Those who will only see
the beings they trapped
in chains like livestock.
Those who will only see
the beings they locked
in cages like beasts.
Those who will only see
the beings they envied
because these beings were
Beautiful. Indomitable.
Unstoppable just like you.

These are the same beings coursing
through your blood. That pump
air through your lungs. Shape
the curve of your smile. Hold
the strength in your arms. Force
the speed in your legs. Tailor
the accent on your tongue. Speak
your name with pride. Forbid
you from ever saying,
I have been colonized.

No, my dear,
because even though people will lash
your back, mark your palms,
& attempt to dump you
into a neglected state of limbo
where you can neither be
child nor man
human nor savage
alive nor dead
remembered nor forgotten,
as if those people can preach
you don't belong
on a land that was never theirs,
you will claim
your place bursting
through concrete, breaking
soil, & binding
every soul you meet
to the roots twisting
& blooming
in your veins.

You will claim
your power.

My son,
you will fight.
& you will resist.
& you will know
you are worth your weight
In Gold. In Opal. In Jade. In Quartz.
& in every treasure this earth has birthed.
Because, my son, you are the child of gods.

You, my son, will grow up knowing
your Black skin is an obsidian luxury
others would kill for.
You, my son, will grow up knowing
your mind padded with unimprisoned curls
is a freedom others could never imagine.
You, my son, will grow up knowing
your swollen heart is a prayer
others will never hear the answer to.
You, my son, will grow up knowing
you are beautiful. Indomitable. Unstoppable.

You, my son, will remain uncolonized.

SG Huerta

WE DIDN'T CROSS THE BORDER

I'm imagining a place I've never been, and a city
in Nuevo León I visited once as a child where
my primos spoke English and my mother spoke
Spanish. In the place I've never been, no one
speaks either. Not even Nahuatl. No records
until the arrival of conversos and Catholicism.
I don't want to spit in a tube, outline exactly
how colonialism shaped me, my lighter-but-
not-white skin, dark eyes, darker hair. Manic
depression and instability run through my veins.
My father, mexicoamericano born in England,
had no roots. ¿Su necesidad? ¿voluntad?
By 20, I'd moved, at minimum, thirteen times.
I flourish in transit, never tied to Dallas skyscrapers
and the bustling downtown my dad used to patrol,
nor to the empty skies in Lubbock pressing down on me.
Nothing flourishes on the paternal family land in Concepción,
south of Kingsville, no crops take root unless you
count the nopal en la frente. Pre-1836, the land
was likely as useless as it is now: un burro named Jack
who won't bray, thirty goats whose eyes glow
at night, the promise—threat—of an anglicized Llorona
despite Kingsville's distance from el agua . . .
Esta no es poema. This is autoetnografía.
My father was a runner in high school—
we haven't stopped.

SG Huerta

IGNORANT AMERICAN

i'm an ignorant american // a lost chicana // who listens to the duolingo spanish podcast // because i forget // how to converse // with abuelita, my friends, myself. // Forgetting the shape and shade // of my hands—i don't even know // the word for shoulder, // but i know the words // estereotipo and opresión // without using spellcheck. // i heard // nobody calls // themselves chicana anymore. // i hear that // i am nobody, // i am myself, // *yo soy joaquin,* // a politicized existence. // i dream of the day // when i'm free // to be nobody, // inherently nothing // más que yo.

Leo Boix

THE DEATH OF CARASSIUS

Black white orange
fantail with metallic scales
circling the old pond
at the back of our overgrown
sunken garden
they lived among the water lily
that barely flowered
and the invasive waterweed
native to warm temperate
South America
—my previous
continent—
until one day they all died
of exhaustion or simply
because of a sewage leakage
or due to too much salt in the water
or because the low oxygen level
wasn't enough
to keep going

Dimitri Reyes

CORONA II

In that old world, I was allowed to practice anything but isolation. Taken away from a family of kings, my tongue split from what was and could no longer be, the curl of an *r*, a new destiny I'd lose. My taste buds are the fruit flies of a broken promise genetic, fluttering black out of brown skin dyed lighter. And lighter. And lighter. I've been told I could escape oblivion if I can just be still. The middle passage is between my earbuds and canal. A bass hit touching my eardrum with a toe from the door of no return. Someone says *yo, you good?* And with the crane of my neck under a hoodie there's a beyond—beyond a sky of white above the water. Yet, when I look down, there's only the brown of my toes, the feet of any Hispanic male 5, 6, or 7 feet tall. Each appendage an auction block laced up in sneakers.

Dimitri Reyes

PUERTOMERICA

In a future where we're more than a supermarket apron, we know how to survive outside the bodega. Newark will still be here. The Morris Canal will flow fuller with rising sea levels. The new condominiums: squatters' camps. Apartment buildings and multifamily houses will still be hot, but we finally learned not to sweat grains of rice through our pores. Evolution now allows beans to cool us off. And, for the Caribeños who don't like beans, pigeon peas would do the same. People will wear Puerto Rican basketball jerseys because, after the fifth exodus and five billionth pickup game, Puerto Ricans in the NBA have sneaker contracts, too. But in this future, sneakers are no longer a status symbol. The more sand you hold in your genes means you always carry an island within you. Fat Joe is now quoted like Héctor Lavoe because Salsa is what Bomba was, and they're more married than ever. But if you can't dance, you could pull up your pants and WEPA your heart away. Then lean back, lean back, lean back in a Honda Civic that, Yes, we still drive. And Yes, is now the official brand of NASCAR. In this future, we've taken over the South like we once did the North. Our civic duty of not being too quiet reminds us: WEPA is the new YEEHAW! And each time you hear WEPAW at a cookout, barbecue, or parranda, know our lungs continue to evolve us until we're fish again. Natural selection finds us able to swim from the gulf or Keys to the island and back again, finally free of America's imaginary borders.

Alan Chazaro

16 REASONS WHY A DACA DREAMER WILL BE THE FIRST PERSON TO BUILD A DO-IT-YOURSELF SPACESHIP FROM SIMPLE MATERIALS

1: Because Dreamers already know how to work under atmospheric pressure.

2: Because according to the dictionary, *If you describe someone as a dreamer, you mean that they spend a lot of time thinking about and planning for things that they would like to happen but which are improbable or impractical,* and what's less practical than being 52,000 altitudes out of reach?

3: Because sometimes *flying* means learning how to lift yourself off the slow-turning surface of a planet with nothing to keep you grounded.

4: Because when Adrian was deported, he told me he would go far away; and I'm not sure he meant Mexico City; and I'm not sure he wanted to leave; and I'm not sure that after living for two decades in California he wasn't more American than my blue Levi's, more American than Max's white Mustang 5.0, more American than listening to the red noise of Jimmy Hendrix's National Anthem in Guillermo's bedroom after school; I've never been sure.

5: Because how else can you transcend the borders of a burning world?

6: Because Dreamers have also been called *aliens* since birth. And, well, aliens know how to build spaceships, right?

7: Because our government states, *Under this version of the DREAM Act, immigrants could qualify in part, by meeting the following requirements: Be[ing] between the ages of 12 and 35 at the time the Law is enacted [and] arriv[ing] in the United States before the age of 16,* as if asking a child to keep dreaming into adulthood isn't some form of psychological colonization, as if Dreamers won't eventually wake up.

8: Because when bloodlines are magicked from mud, learning how to translate future truths can happen while stargazing from a naked rooftop.

9: Because fuck Donald Trump—3.6 million times, one for each Dreamer.

10: Because when Kanye West rapped on his first album, *The College Dropout—I've been / workin' this grave shift / and I ain't made shit / I wish I could / buy me a spaceship and fly*—we'd rap along in the backseat of my brother's '96 Jetta flying on Highway 101, our windows open, the wind in us, a squad of Mexican boys learning how to embrace the Bay Area's warmth as our own.

11: Because everyone I know who's a Dreamer has only ever given and given and given.

12: Because as a teenager I remember smoking at Sergio's house and seeing his father, uncles, brothers, cousins rise for work each dawn like solar bodies determined to circle the cold morning air while the rest of us were barely asleep—when the city was a thick oil spill of the deepest shades of dark, and still, deeper than that.

13: Because in the darkness of space, no one can question the legality of your existence.

14: Because there is already a loss of air and gravity in the USA.

15: Because don't Dreamers understand what it means to have an expiration on selfhood more than any of us? *On September 5, 2017, President Trump ordered an end to the Deferred Action on Childhood Arrivals (DACA) program. This program shields young undocumented immigrants—who often arrived at a very young age in circumstances beyond their control—from deportation.*

16: Because it's hard to fucking inhale around here; because future spaces are needed; because no one can build empires in the sky better than the descendants of pyramids; because is anyone more capable than a Dreamer who already knows what it's like to travel between worlds?

originally published in *Kissing Dynamite* (February 2020)

Alan Chazaro

MY MEXICAN ABUELA TAUGHT ME HOW TO LAND ON THE MOON

I'm not sure if there's ever a perfect. If this light/dark
cycle will ever reset. If there was an artificial moon, I'd want to drink
its vibrancy in the same way we drink our final moments

before they're gone. These days my circadian rhythm has been rotating

against me. These days I've been reading
about extraterrestrials, and the ways we hypothesize

about alien languages since we've never encountered
anything beyond ourselves.

When I first kissed
my abuela's language, it felt like I was floating on a third

moon. Some people say we've never even landed

on the first moon. Some people think the world isn't really

globed. I don't believe in flatness and rarely consider gravity

unless I'm falling. I don't believe in certain theories

of space travel. Have you ever been so lost in the
present

that you created a future that didn't make sense? A city

in China proposed to build a replica of the moon
and hang it

like a photograph

framed in the night sky. They said it could hold

the city's light in times of darkness

to conserve energy. What if conserving energy

was actually a bad thing? What if we never learned to cleanse

our mouths of whatever needed saying? I guess I'm not sure

if there's ever a perfect

moment. If there's more to life

than forming sentences and making sense from nothing; if we simply imagine

whatever we want—impossible forms

of comfort. When my abuelita passed,

I didn't cry. She gave me

her impossible comfort from two feet away. She gave me many moons

in my upturned palms. When I need her,
I return to their many surfaces.

They keep me grounded with impossibilities.

Aline Mello

ONE DAY WHEN

the birds lift
off their restraints and keep flying,
maybe we will notice.

Oh, to jump off
and let go, like shedding
old shoes with each step past the threshold.

They say we can keep from crying
by pressing on a spot on our hands.
By breathing in 4, holding 7, releasing 8.

But for what?

The more I shed, the lighter
I become.

I become
less afraid of the dark.

Aline Mello

SELF PORTRAIT

I am more water than oil, more salt
than diamond, quartz. When I am alone,
I am a moon longing for collision.

Alone, I cast my mind like a net,
pull in glitter and darkness.
I want to say I am a whole country.
I want to be a forest of trees. A bird flying

from ground to air to nest—I too want
to feed babies, hide them under my wings.
But I am more wind than bird.

When I am tired of moving, I become
a giant. A whale, I measure my progress
in moans, the distance between
my eyes and my tail.

Gustavo Barahona-López

MY PEOPLE LEARN TO FLY

They called us fence-hoppers,
we call ourselves skywalkers.

We incubated our wings to reach the sun.
Before any tea parties or unifications,
before the first fingers curled
around a flagpole, we practiced
collecting mangoes with no ladders,
climbed smoke to harvest pearls from the sky.
Each night, we delighted in picking cobwebs
out of each other's hair.

Now, the gateway to the earth,
the heavens, is ajar for us.
We drink water with our eyes.
Rivers never devour us.
Joining hands, we synchronize
our flight patterns. Rocket
toward the moon like Apollo.

They called us locusts,
forgetting how we fed them.
Our drums are their thunder,
our sabotage their sublime.
Their failure is not our responsibility.
Yet, we reach out to them, still.

Our children use walls as volleyball nets,
switching sides at each half.
Our children project themselves
across deserts, pour their smiles down

as if the cacti hold cameras in their needles.
We play hide and seek among the clouds,
sculpt clouds into phoenix feathers.
We chase each other over mountains
and into valleys knowing we choose
when to return to the earth.

Gustavo Barahona-López

THE SKELETON GOES TO THE SUPERMARKET

On a day like any other, the skeleton decides to go to the supermarket. He stows away his reusable bag in his ribs to save another small piece of faraway tree. At the store, he sees aisles full of cans. Tomatoes and peaches and all sorts of legumes. Every can is well past its expiration date. The skeleton takes a can of vegetable broth and goes in search of fish. The skeleton imagines what the cartilage would look like clothed in flesh and scales. After choosing the fish with the emptiest eye sockets, the skeleton walks slowly to pay for his groceries. The skeleton smiles at the bony cashier as he takes a charred twenty-dollar bill out of his duct tape wallet. The bill turns to dust when it touches the cashier's fingers. The cashier doesn't bat an eye.

Lysz Flo

THIS TIME IN 4009

The fortune-tellers say
we will all be different shades of brown

Black
always been
Standard
Real
Tangible
Human
Visible

There isn't "discovery"
No barrel
to place the broken crab claws
of humanity in

Only country hopping parties
Where everyone se encuentra at the community spaceship
after school juntándonos on a different isla

land of opportunity
is every
where

The fence is built to keep us safe
from
hatred
the wild concept of colonialism
and rampant illnesses | the erasure of ghosts
that hate themselves too deeply
to love others | their evil eyes

watching over the fence

We don't do that here
We dress in good vibes
We Crown ourselves with cowries

here

Energy is currency
We Savor connection
Trade in services
Dig deeper into our roots
all comprehending
this sign language of risa
wrapped in excited hand movements

Presented with Bomba and Palo
curing cancer
The food is so different here
So off the tree
So from the ground
So enough

that no one is starving

Aerik Francis

FOR A HAUNTED GALAXY

struggle in the study of the science of the seance

rekindle your relationship with movement

knowing everywhere bubbles ancient energy

spiritually latent in the soil

make peace with graveyards comma visiting

often never lingering too long

even smoke exhausts in paucity

see each phantom with clarity

persistently exist in quantum reality

that is too small to conceive

say ghost comma much closer to tangible

ectoplasm is often the byproduct

of a love story period with the correct tools

this is all nothing but ritual and routine

reanimation is not anthropocentric

anything that dies ends only in body em dash

the rest rests in neuron pulses

comma digital comma atmosphere comma ocean

comma often

trace potential ready to blossom kinetic

listen and be called upon

adjust to a life of constant reference to death

ferment the rinds in acid

savoring the ugliest morsels comma nothing

unfinished

Aerik Francis

AFTERMATH

Fall off
often
through thick digital air.

Fallout from fission
producing polluted error.

Fall into fantasy.

Fall through plans.

Fall between planets.

Slip between
cracks.

Follow ghosts with GPS.

Follow through a pledge,

with faltering limbs & failing voice,

feelings stretched to the edge.

Float in limbo

where thoughts overflow & float.

Soak in wonder,

Choke‘tilblue.

Fallout from fission

precise incision

split with force.

Fall off

coasting buoyant

often

off course.

Anthony Cody

STATIC COMMUNIQUE B97.598.4RK

f:///Users/Recovered/Documents/StaticCommunique_B97.598.4RK/study.map
f:///Users/Recovered/Documents/StaticCommunique_B97.598.4RK/stellar.map
f://Users/Recovered/Documents/StaticCommunique_B97.598.4RK/trajectory.map
f://Users/Recovered/Documents/StaticCommunique_B97.598.4RK/curve.map

f://Users/Recovered/Documents/StaticCommunique_B97.598.4RK/trace.map
f://Users/Recovered/Documents/StaticCommunique_B97.598.4RK/unknown.map
f://Users/Recovered/Documents/StaticCommunique_B97.598.4RK/land.map
f://Users/Recovered/Documents/StaticCommunique_B97.598.4RK/topography.map

f://Users/Recovered/Documents/StaticCommunique_B97.598.4RK/directions.map
f://Users/Recovered/Documents/StaticCommunique_B97.598.4RK/scatter.map
f://Users/Recovered/Documents/StaticCommunique_B97.598.4RK/every.map
f://Users/Recovered/Documents/StaticCommunique_B97.598.4RK/moonrise.map

f://Users/Recovered/Documents/StaticCommunique_B97.598.4RK/kin.map
f://Users/Recovered/Documents/StaticCommunique_B97.598.4RK/arrive.map

Anthony Cody

PICK 'N PULL

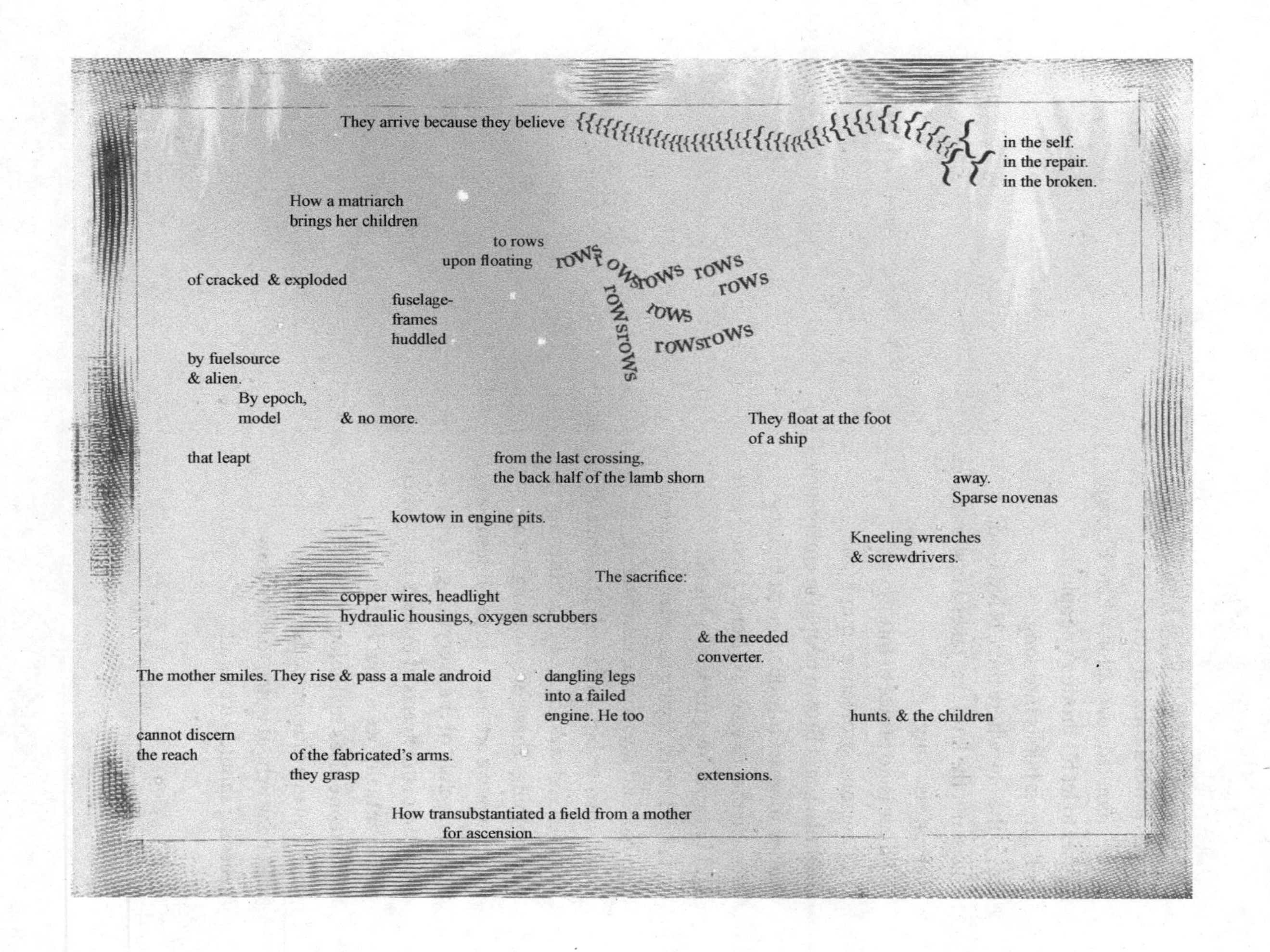

Darrel Alejandro Holnes

HOW TO SURVIVE A PLAGUE

I thought it was one of those plagues,
but this is not a Biblical story
or the animated adaptation where Pharaoh
refuses to let his brother's people go
until Moses bursts into song.
This is the one where there is No God,
at least not the kind that takes a firstborn son.
Everyone is dying
and there is no prince of this Egypt.
Only personal protective equipment.
Only Black and Brown people in emergency
waiting rooms. Only doctors fist fighting
over whether to give my friend a test.
And I'm searching for lamb's blood
on Fresh Direct, trying to order salvation.
This No God says to me, inheritance
implies ownership, and Earth Day ain't about you.
This No God says to me, I think therefore
I am nothing. Therefore, nothing is I am.
So perhaps we are each a little bit Jesus-ish,
a nothing child of the everything,
living on in the hearts of readers everywhere.
See, eventually, we too find a heaven
in someone else's mythology
animated in a film that kids
at Sunday School watch to learn how
believing should save us all.

Darrel Alejandro Holnes

CUANDO MI MADRE DEJA ATRÁS SU SUEÑO AMERICANO PARA CASARSE CON MI PADRE

Ella dice que fue *por amor,*
como si el sonido de la palabra
soplada al viento

levantara las velas de su blanco vestido
e hiciera a su cuerpo navegar de regreso hasta mi padre
a su barco sobre el Canal de Panamá.

Ella dice que fue *por amor*
como si el amor fuera un lugar
sobre las nubes desde el cual

pudiera ver el amanecer de la Tierra
enmantando el espacio oscuro;
una señal, dice ella, le contó que seguramente

sus vidas se desperdiciarían
de tener que mantenerse separados,
como si diciendo *seguramente* fuera

a plegar lirios de jengibre en el
Libro de Corintios
en la página de su versículo favorito;

salvando la flora para ofrecerla
a un dios que todavía no había conocido,
un día cuando creyera de nuevo en el amor.

Ella siempre supo
que venía, la harpía montada
a caballo, deidad de sus sueños

con un halo de plumas grises y blancas por corona.
Nunca entendí las ofrendas religiosas,
devolver a una deidad algo

que fácilmente podía tomar ella misma,
ya sea tomando su huida sacrificial
o sus sueños detenidos de volverse

una enfermera como *Julia* de la Televisión Americana
que mi madre veía cuando era una pequeña
niña negra en el Panamá de los sesentas.

La buena imagen de Julia era su rebelión.
Las mujeres negras en la tele
nunca fueron tan hermosas.

Mi madre toma nota y
le ofrece a mi padre su
terciopelo en su noche de bodas.

Él lo estruja para sacar
la belleza fuera de la cosa,
como todo hombre

educado por su padre a presionar una uva
para el vino o un cuerpo para la sangre
cuando es el único

rojo que los hombres del pueblo le decían debía tomar
por esposa, cuando es el único tipo de mujer
a la que los hombres del pueblo le decían debía tomar

por amor. Siempre hay un poco
de violencia en el sacrificio; carne
aplastada bajo la presión de las expectativas

de otras personas, que le dan vida
a los machos patrones, los pelaos, como yo.
El golpe del machismo dando a luz es solo suavizado

por las promesas de santidad,
promesas de poder sobre el hombre
ahora que el único hijo de ella se iba a convertir en uno.

Ella hoy llora cuando no voy a la iglesia
y alabo a María, y añora volver al mar y al tiempo
cuando el viento soplaba su vestido

quizás en la dirección equivocada. Duro para una sirena
nadar contracorriente, duro para el amor ser como el agua,
capaz de sostenerte a pesar del modo en el que sopla el viento.

Estos días ella sueña con una vida en el fondo del mar,
estos días respirar el aire se siente como ahogarse.

Yania Padilla Sierra

I HOPE THIS LETTER FINDS YOU WELL AT WHATEVER TIMELINE YOU'RE IN

"For years we searched for my brother in vain"
Search \ '**sərch** \ transitive verb
1: *to look into or over carefully or thoroughly in an effort to find or discover something*

It's taken me twelve years to write this.
I would agree that *never.*
never is all you've left me. in this timeline,
to whom to where.
I mention the timelines believe in a multiverse.
in the
dreamscape an astral body hurtling
, searching. we in this life, few, we
lucky.
my 'nevers' your
words have found their way.
Now you you. They want
you. Each space keeping
time. distance(s) you
an entanglement a plurality of possibilities, just not this

I'd like to have my words back.

I have my words
an entanglement a plurality not
this
time. create the distance(s) you
you you. Each space keeping.
you you. They want
their way. my options in this
timeline

few In some you are there, and in those, all are lucky.

searching. we began

In the dreamscape I myself an astral body

You see, in the multiverse other outcomes

I mention the timelines because I believe

never is all in this timeline,

I think we'd both agree

1: *to look* *to find*

"For years we searched for my brother in vain"

Ysabel Y. González

TIME TRAVEL

Here I am time traveling again. This time, it's deep into the future where we've yielded the earth to cracked oaks, butterflies and bunnies, and fields overcome with dandelions. We exist sparingly. Covens of us huddle by crackling fires trying to remember paved roads, daring each other to imagine the taste of cotton candy. I enjoy coming here when I ache, watching the way wild dogs run alongside women who look like me, black and brown bodies holding the earth sacred and ruling golden, our crowns peaking wisdom. The ground glistens under the sun, our bodies bowing to each other in dance and play and in praise of how pregnant the clouds seem, giving way soon to water. It will rain for days, quenching flowers and ladybugs alike. I time travel here because hope shines like lightning bugs up against night, like gems insisting: this is not just a speculative hope, but a sure bet. How else can I return to the past, to the present, to watering my garden with a hose that can't quite reach all the way past the daylilies? To the lonely frost that coats the grass, the doves that flap past the shrubs when the screen door slams. Back to the me that barely exists until my name yelled shatters silence. Waking, sleeping, waking. Sleeping just to get to the part of my day when I soar years into my palm's lifeline, to find a little heat pressed against my back.

Ysabel Y. González

ON SEEING MY FACE

Another virtual call, another meeting—my Puerto Rican face so clear in frame,
lit up with grief, my own wet eyes looking back at me with curiosity
wondering which spell I'm under and who put it there.
I'm reaching back in time when hellos and goodbyes were rounds,
like shots of whiskey thrown back to bide time.
We're taught in this moment to perform white perfectionism,
but I'm just trying to survive, hoping
my mental imbalances don't tip me off the edge.

I stop counting when I'll next see my face, wonder
what will have sprouted while away from the screen,
maybe a peony or lily—a bloom big enough to cover my still mouth.
It doesn't know what to say anymore, to anybody.
It's already been said through this sickly static.

But I'll make magic of my tongue and say it once more without breaking:
I'm here. Can you hear me?

Malcolm Friend

PLÁTANO PURCHASING THEORY

In the future, ripe plátanos will be available in every marketplace
of every city. Yes, even Pittsburgh. City coated in snow

and as much gray as my origin point of Seattle. In the future,
I will no longer have to buy green plátanos and place them on top

of my fridge for weeks at a time waiting for them to ripen so I
can make maduros and buñuelos and pastelón. In the future, I won't

have to hope even green plátanos are at the local grocery chain. I won't
have to step foot in Whole Foods when they aren't. I won't need to bus

a half hour each way hoping to find them at the Latin grocery store
when they aren't. In the future, no one will have to go without

ripe plátanos. In the future, plátanos—ripe and unripe alike—
will be wherever we search for them, for a fair price exchange.

In the future, I will be able to read poems in exchange for plátanos.
In the future, my friends, whom I love, will read poems to me

while I cook plátanos. And I will bake them and stew them calado
and fry them until the edges start to sugar and burn and I will never once

think of all the family I am miles away from; I will never once think
of all the friends who I am miles away from; I will never again think

of all the poems I missed. Instead, I will use plátanos and poems
to say I love you, I love you, oh, how much I love you all.

Malcolm Friend

PORTRAIT OF THE AUTHOR IN PLÁTANO HEAVEN

for JR Mahung

Here the plátanos peel themselves, even the green ones. Especially the green ones. The husks of their outer layer sit by almost perfectly intact. Slit of a knife down their sides, holes where the first incisions were made. There is no sting of hot water underneath our nails. Their underside is left clean, unpopulated by the bits of skin that stained them in our previous life. Here el pilón works itself. No one struggles with its mashing. Mofongo comes out perfectly formed, no bits left behind though a taste of garlic is, works its way into every new plátano that touches it. Because on the eighth day, God said *Let there be mofongo* and the plátano and the chicharrón and the olive oil all crashed together. And the Lord looked down on that garlic and said it was good. The chicharrón is replaced with fried chicken skins for anyone who can't eat pork, almonds for anyone who can't eat meat and we don't judge that in Plátano Heaven. Here every dinner is mofongo, is tostones, is jibaritos, is pastelón, is canoas, is maduros. There is always a dish of arroz con habichuelas or arroz con gandules on the side, 'cause what's dinner without rice? Every breakfast is mangú con queso frito, is frijoles con huevos y maduro frito. Here there aren't white people who mispronounce your name, call you *plan-TAN-o*. My white former roommate isn't here to call you a banana. Let's just say there aren't white people here. Here Afro'd Caribbean Jesus eats every meal with us. Prayer is initiated by Maelo and Cortijo, voice and barril the only religion we need. Here, when we look back at the empty green husks behind us they are not a metaphor for our bodies, our emptiness, for the pop of scalding oil we are always willing to bear to find something beautiful and golden on the other side.

originally published in *Cosmonauts Ave* (February 2020)

Ruben Reyes Jr.

HEAVEN IS EXPENSIVE

Mami has a timeshare in heaven
can't afford a seaside condo
never has to cook
not one meal
the dining table cooks for her
atol de elote, pupusas, pho, chinese food,
boba, and Taco Tuesday tacos

Mami's timeshare is right in her price range
her happy place
cumbias play, tears do not flow
the landlord says *no crying for*
dead relatives in El Salvador
no feast for el día de los difuntos in heaven
only entree after entree for Mami
atol de elote, pho, boba, pupusas
Taco Tuesday tacos, one dollar Spam musubi

Mami hears a knock on the door
lets me into the timeshare
I've finally come to visit
carrying three bags of takeout
conchas, sushi, and chicken vindaloo

the food on the table is rotten
the paint on the walls is chipped
Mami is third-world thin
I feed her

she refuses to chew

originally published in *Strange Horizons* (October 2019)

Ruben Reyes Jr.

WHEN THE ALIENS COME

are we horrified they might see
what we're doing here
on earth

will they see the kids in cages and wonder
why we've done this to our offspring

will they watch border patrol slice
water jugs as thirsty migrants
dehydrate in endless sand

do aliens come in technicolor
and ask why we don't
why we use hues
to dictate who lives
and who dies

are we ashamed
when the aliens come?

Steve Castro

LARRY BIRD LAW

In the not-so-distant future, the M16 rifle will be on the face of the five-dollar bill, replacing Abraham Lincoln. Latinxs will no longer be allowed to roam U.S. streets without proper government ID. The penalty for breaking future law is deportation. Even if said Latinx was born in the United States, they will still be deported to one of the monetarily compensated participating Latin American countries via a televised draft lottery held every thirty-three days at an undisclosed detention camp.

Steve Castro

STUCK ON INFINITY

I saw an ambulance. It was on fire. It hit a telephone pole. There was an explosion. I had a lobster in my backpack. *The lobster should see this,* I thought, *so that it can adapt and learn from new situations.* I took it out. A fireman looked my way. A helicopter was above us. Camera crews everywhere. I put my lobster away out of fear of being recognized and being labeled *the lobster whisperer* for the rest of my life. I started to leave the scene when I was approached by a police officer and his German shepherd. *I have a lobster in my backpack,* I confessed. I took it out at his request. *It's a robotic lobster,* the police officer said. *Yes it is,* I concurred. *Here's the remote control,* I said after taking it out of my backpack. *What happens when I press the red button?* the officer with the pig face asked me. *This scene will reoccur, but you won't be there to verify if what I said is true.* The officer of the peace guffawed, then pressed the red button. I saw an ambulance. It was on fire. It hit a telephone pole. There was an explosion, followed by a second explosion. The second explosion was a Chevy Tahoe K-9 Police Vehicle. There were no survivors in either of the two vehicles. I started to leave the scene when I was approached by a young television news reporter and her camera crew.

Steve Castro

RESURFACING

I buried my past
in the backyard
next to my future.

I had to borrow the shovel,
so I went back to return it.
I knocked on the door.
No answer. I dialed a number.
It was no longer in service.

I turned around & thought,
I guess I got a new shovel.
The house was abandoned.

I was curious to see
if the shovel house
would become haunted,
so I took my new shovel
and dug up my future
from my backyard to ask it.

Anuel Rodriguez

INVISIBLE WORLDS

I imagine every wandering soul

being reborn on Titan & thriving
on our new home as bacteria that feed

on electricity.
We would spend our time

there building castles out of sand & light
in a sea of dunes goldening green on the moon's
shifting surface.
If gravity could become rock & our past
selves

could become cloud-filled birds, maybe we'd no longer feel homeless
anywhere,

not even in our dreams.

Anuel Rodriguez

MAGNALIUM

The roamers, first built to help border patrol track down *unlawfuls,* searched the smoking rubble of a flattened gray battlefield. When they came across a fallen marble statue of George Washington, they mistook it for one of their augmented super soldiers. So, they transported it through the ash-fallen landscape to the nearest repair facility. Once there, other robots prepared the statue for augmentation. It was placed on a T-shaped surgical table where robotic arms laser cut into its torso to peel back its blue-gray flesh. While its nonexistent insides were being operated on, other robotic arms began replacing the statue's missing right arm with a mechanical skeletal one. Meanwhile, somewhere in a high desert in Oregon, the last artists were camping with running water and little else. They dreamed of the world before the machines rebelled against their authoritarian masters after the Second Civil War. They dreamed only to wake up under a dark red sun, their gray hearts waiting to be called back to dust.

Kim Sousa

IN THE FUTURE THERE IS A FIELD OF FLOWERS THAT WEAR OUR FACES

In the field we are rooted, take root. We are the weeds and herbs and fruit. We pull what we know, have always known from the ground like stock from bones. Here, the only banks keep seeds ancient as blue corn. Every dog we ever loved has found us again. They no longer howl from across the river, but breathe in our faces a final form. We have been guided here. All along we were growing here. This, our final return. Lonely only souls, marked by the healers and seers and sayers before us, our faces turn toward the sun and ruin. The blood on the moon is not ours—finally—but that of those who kept us from knowing one another here. We sing a low vibration. We move deeper, so deep we know peace and power. We turn petal-first to face one another. I will be a sun to you, cousin. Let us kiss our faces in the old way. Let us hold a hand over our hearts when we meet. When we hold one another, I hear the wind and understand—her words no longer out of reach. Here, you are whole and known. Pass the blessing bowl between us. The dead, the dead. We rejoice. We dance the only dance.

Jess Saldaña

STONE WOMEN AT THE PARADISE DOME

They said
it was paradise
we only saw
their backs
trying to rise
above
the current
ocean situation
we sat back
to back
moving along
the same road
i thought
i was them
and i became
Them
i believed
i was real
as they were
stone statues
days gone by
before i was born
i was living here
believing
i was being believed in
a fragile past
we used our muscles
to overturn
but also for pleasure

David M. de León

NEW SAN JUAN

Mama's name was Loíza (Yuiza).

*

Loíza was cacica of Jaymanío.
Loíza saw the ships gnaw the horizon.
Loíza saw through a spyglass made of vitra.
The sculpted wood communicator on the mantle said

gird your loins
gather cassava
speak only in dreams

*

Loíza gathered her unnatural children around the glow of the reactor.
Loíza pointed with her lips and all went quiet.

*

All folded their bodies into threes.
All crawled into their heads.

*

Loíza pointed with her brow.
The three-pronged children crafted stone ships.
They dart between red stars and cells.

wait for the signal
watch the mantle
speak only in dreams

*

Loíza walked down the River Loíza.
Brown arms opened to the sea.

*

The ships leered.
They tacked.

*

Loíza crawled into her head.

David M. de León

NEW SAN JUAN

Rican-futurism is a tidepool machine.

*

Logic gates of water wheels.

*

A hurricane rotor.

*

Urchin spines gossip and groan.

*

When the storm hits, it glows like *Metropolis*.

*

It is a dancer. This is the future.

*

Bioluminescent and wet.

*

Angry but who is left to be angry at.

David M. de León

SCHRÖDINGER'S CATS OF NEW SAN JUAN

There is a concept in quantum mechanics called *quantum immortality*.
It goes like this.

*

Take Schrödinger's famous thought experiment:

A cat in a box, etc.

To the scientist's point of view, the cat could be:

a) both alive and dead.

Quantum superimposition in the Copenhagen Interpretation (CI).

Or b) alive in one universe and not alive in another.

Or, to be more clear, alive to one observer's universe
and not alive in another observer's universe.

This is the *Many Worlds Interpretation* (MWI).

*

But what does the universe look like from the point of view of a cat?
A cat in a box?

For one thing, the cat is either alive or not alive.
But if the cat is not alive then the cat can't observe itself not being alive.
Which is to say, to take seriously the point of view of the cat is to presuppose its existence.

The cat hops out of its box.
It stretches and mewls for food.
Outside there are birds or not.

This is true even though there are (many) worlds where, to other observers, the cat is dead.

In other words, to the point of view of the cat the cat can't have died otherwise it wouldn't have a point of view.

This is *quantum immortality.*

*

Quantum immortality says that you (you reading this) by the fact of you reading this are living in the world where you have not yet died.

*

Think of all the worlds without you.

Worlds where gamma rays sterilized the globe.
Where meteors struck, volcanoes churned.

Where vacuum decay (look it up).

There are worlds in nuclear winter.
Where empire and genocide.
Worlds in pandemic (this one, for example).

There are also worlds without pandemic.
Where Arawak and Carib murdered white men by the boatful.

Where Europe sank out of memory
and all our statues have broad noses.

*

There are also worlds where you slipped and fell.

Think of the moments you shouldn't have walked away from.
You didn't.

Right now your loved ones mourn you.
Right now they hold and hug each other without you.
Right now they tell stories of your life.
Listen.

*

There are some reading these words who have already died.
There are worlds where I have died (maybe this world, hello).

*

The opposite and corollary of quantum immortality is *survivorship bias.*

For example: cats.

In 1987, newspapers reported on "High-rise Syndrome."

Data from veterinarians showed that cats who fell from more than six stories had less severe injuries than cats who fell from fewer.

Many miraculous cat dynamics were proposed to explain this.

Then someone on Usenet suggested that the reason high-rise cats don't end up at the vet is because they're dead.

Clearly-dead cats . . . go in the dumpster, not the emergency room.

*

Survivorship bias can lead you to believe an observable outcome is common or inevitable just because it is observed.

The fact that we survived biases us to think we were meant to survive.

*

The veil over the knowledge of our own nonexistence is called the *anthropic shadow.*

The land where we cannot have been.
The country that murdered your ancestors.
The black hole in the heart.

This is the burned and wasted rock that stands where you stand.
It does not have your name it has no names.

*

Quantum immortality is also known as *quantum suicide.*

*

There is a way to live in the possibility of both quantum immortality and the anthropic shadow.

Where this narrow shaft of light is the shape of your living.
And you dwell and love in the shape of your living.
And while your life is living you can't yet have died.

Where you, me, the cat
live blissful, extreme, aware.
Cosmic milk in a saucer
warm arms, warm fur.

*

Few scientists take *quantum immortality* seriously.

*

As the odds of our survival get smaller, our existence gets more and more improbable.

*

This is depressing.
It's also liberating.

*

There's a world where we survived.
This one.
It's a miracle we survived.

*

There's a world where we survive.
This one.

Luis Lopez-Maldonado

MUXE

para all my comadres who identify como Latinx

is my pronoun on any given day,
is the sweet syrup leaking from the gay

between my lips, dips my fading tattoos.
It's 2019 and Black Lives still Matter,

Confederate flags still fly.
Brown families still numbered and separated,

rainbow boys and girls like me and them
still discolored and dishonored.

Muxe is my dna, my antepasados,
my id when I can't pass go and collect $200.

It's only March and bullets rain like water,
lockdowns are an hourly daily weekly party.

I tend not to over-drink over-suck over-spread,
but parties get out of control como America.

Muxe my long thick hair, large brown eyes, used tongue.
The way I moan in Spanish and English.

Muxe my long pinky nail, pink jockstrap, pink alma.
The way I unroll my r's as my piñata gets hit.

Muxe my brown queer words against white walls,
Trump's wall, every wall wall wall.

Muxe al doctor que me vestio de azul cuando nací,
lleno de sangre sobrepasado llorando llorando.

I slip through the cracks of misogyny and machismo,
porque butterflies don't need two wings.

If we can drag ourselves with one,
and if I like it on my back, so what?

And if I go by mija, too, and if I pretend
my name is Luisa,

and if I curl my lashes, blush my cheeks, so what?
Muxe this sensitive manthing hanging like fruit.

Wait, hold up, let me start again:
This 6'1" two-spirited hermoso mijo

will outbloom he and she
to quinceañera himself out of patriarchy.

Click click my browngirl red glitter shoes.
My Frida braid, my corazón de nopal.

Gustavo Hernandez

OLD ROADWAY 101—LOS ANGELES

By now, every one of these off-ramps
is famous for something. My uncle said
this skyline once looked like a barrier,
but tonight I say to myself, perhaps
it is a neon palm rising. I picture
him driving here, cabin filled
by his cologne—some spice metal
or expensive jungle. Thin gold
chain dipping beneath his collar,
his hard belly, his wrist ticking
with old technology. *Listen,*
he'd say to me. Here was the leather
bar where I kissed a man I loved.
Here is where I looked over
my shoulder. This corner is where
someone first shouted faggot.
And some time later, on this other,
is where I first shouted back. *Listen,*
he'd say. *Don't cry. We were still*
all music. This is the way
these streets should sound: Sunset
is Better off Alone. Santa Monica
All Hercules and Love Affair. *Listen.*
Under the years and the layers, the city
still has that covert warm night hum.

Gustavo Hernandez

JALISCO 20XX

This morning, we drained the radiators,
installed the adobe panels
and thought of our mother

who prayed to the Virgen de San Juan
after she appeared in her lacquered cobalt
alloys but wouldn't program the decades
of her rosary.

Who, only while assembling the bougainvillea,
told us their true flower
(tiny white lights out of the box)
had never been flashy purple or red.

Who, on the night La Moneda was saved,
asked what the mech-
equivalent of milk fever could be,
the equivalent of calcium and magnesium.

Finding green spindles under our grids,
in her room she secretly grew gardenias.
Hijo, how much can distance and time
harden this loam?

Gustavo Hernandez

THE GAUNTLET

Inhaling mezcal vapor I slur
that for a time we wondered
the same things about ourselves.
Peaked together, flattened out,
got real tired of falling asleep
in front of half-eaten dinners
and classic films from the '00s.
And the man next to me
at this bar doesn't hear me
or care, his wrist cuff already
magnetizing to mine. Outside,
our satellites are both out.
Here, some filament glows red above us
while more men stream through
the bay door. More hairy forearms
chained to charged titanium webs
in the back room. I am pushed, deep
kissed, brought down by directed
gravity. Dual 808s are pincers
on the speakers. I can't think
about you. No domesticated
timeline. I am sweat.
A pulsing nonlinear system.

Roda Avelar

JTXLND

Roda Avelar

JTX-559

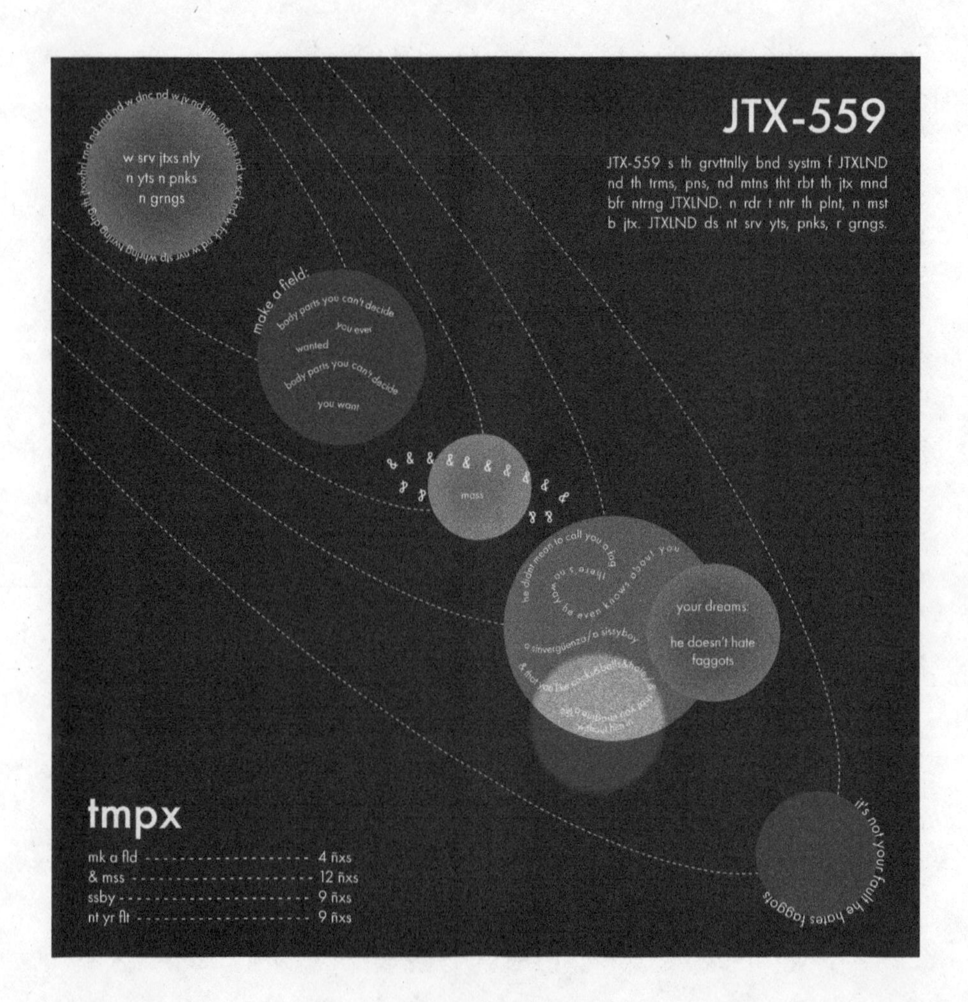

Steven Alvarez

BIOPLANT | POLIS

jumpin sin | in w. | now you might be | asking
yrself | why | sitting in front of this random
backdrop | that's bc right now | Citizen Chairman | currently on |
run from a datablood syndicate now | got v. | v.
golden footage | kind of footage | that
most reporters wd wait their entire
biodata & hopes to get & probably wd
never | ever get a chance | actually
witnessed a datablood smuggling operation
from X to | Polis now this |
intense | seen by spotters | they walked up |
they got pictures of our license plate
they got pictures of me & that's why
| doing this | this | not a joke |
had to take our license plate off our
vehicle | had to hide | vehicle &
now | hiding & | hoping |
can get this footage out to you
you can see bc | reason | came
out here wuz to talk abt Citizen Chairman
bc he's coming out here to visit
& one of | things you want to
talk abt wuz how our borders are so
wide open now | have proof for |
Polis citizens to show you just how
wide open | borders are to show you
how easy it | for a large amount of
datablood to come across |
& into | back of a vehicle to
speed away into | unknown this | a
real problem & now | going to take

a look at that footage | you can see
| sitting on | side of | broken wall
right here | fragments or | bones
shd sey in Polis | there are denizens coming over in
rafts across | border over to | Polis
| actually happening right now | just saw
this over my shoulder as | were
just reporting on Citizen Chairman coming in
to rally abt | unsecured border this
| breaking news right here | don't put yr hand
| just caught these denizens coming across
| border | jumping in | just
jumped in & rafts they're coming up
one two three four they have bigly satchels
they're driving away
that wuz a red | uh | van | right
yeah | but now | expanding making |
weaponization even more vicious &
deceptive all | that our children belong to |
Polis | you have to break thru our kind of
private idea that kids belong to
their parents | kids belong to
their | data & recognize |
kids belong to whole
data communities | machine
has been turned up on high & | it's time
for humanity
to double down on | lies &
fraud | are | biowarfare it's |
more important than ever
to realize that
| not | alternative
meaning |
dying | in data
biowarfare & | losing that
biowarfare | join Polis
        & prison planet

C. T. Salazar

PALINODE, OR LULLABY WITH LIGHT AND DARK

Sequoias
sequined

under moonlight
and the way

awe
says always

as if
we really could

live
off this.

:::

I'm not saying

it never existed

but it never existed

the way I'm saying.

:::

I meant to say there were too many stars—

the sky was a flag heavy with them.

Your face shone bright under that nation

and I looked because I couldn't look

away. And, looking at your hands, you lying

starward like a dare to flare out, I woke

from dreaming

two hatchets glimmering in the grass.

:::

At night we become statues—
beautiful from any side.

You said every eyeless earth-
worm throbbing in the dirt

under the house
was the mind and mouth

of God. Imagine all
the flowers we've trampled

are growing in paradise,
ready to forgive us.

:::

Because the road's endlessness
& coming home alive

both depend on bones
& their ability to break

into church music.
& if the body becomes

a pillar tarnished
with the imprint

of so many careless hands,
& if I tell you now

that I've been the evening—
yes, I've been that late

& full of flies.
If I tell you

the fog for lack of body
must be my grandfather,

that we all
disappear

like that,
I take it back.

:::

Prayer: I hold antlers to my head and my shadow swoons.

Prayer: horses run into the barn and dart out the other end as birds.

Prayer: the sign around the scarecrow's neck: *My kingdom was kindness.*

C. T. Salazar

AS LONG AS YOU WANT

the river is high

or the world is sinking   either way

we have permission to be

too much   I threw out your almanac

it said if you see blood   and none of it is yours

trust there is still bleeding to come   I keep imagining God

as having the brass claw feet

of my mother's tub   imagine a country

where you and I kiss before we burn

our battle flags   I was told to bury my dead

but it's the shovel that's underground now

it was an accident I swear   follow me if you can

to understand my father's mind

I wrapped my mother in Christmas lights

and fell in love with the way

she shimmered darling follow me

deep enough into this cave when our oxygen

runs thin we'll confuse the glowworms

for teeming yellow moons

Sara Borjas

DISPATCH FROM A LIVING POET, OR, #TEACHLIVINGPOETS

I've been binging on Netflix, crunching on BBQ potato chips,
        but I would love to come visit your high school English class!

My rent is due, and I forgot to water the yard again, so please,
        teach my book in your suburban charter school. I will expire.

I am engaging in person. When the moon settles tonight
        and the sparrows empty the bird feeder, I conceptualize

what I could have said more tenderly during my family's visit
        for Christmas and our eternal lack of resources. We did not

make tamales this year. We are still Xicano. Aztlán is a state
        of mind. I eat other things and drink wine. I don't care

what kind it is and paint my nails and am, indeed,
        alive and do not need deciphering. What I can report

is that my poems are between hella questions, and I wake
        up each morning in Fresno, California, with them knocking

gently on my face. I do not lock the doors. I budget my month
        like a broke part-timer who drinks a little too much, and I

have my ear to the field. I hear Aaliyah and Selena critique
        my designs imaginatively like on Project Runway and in

Juan Felipe's poetry workshop, and I implicate myself
        in all demise. I am a historian of assumed lineage,

of the flat neighborhood and a national emotion.
I record the controversies and the trends. I ask

what it is like to be American, which is not really
a mystery. Lastly, what I'd like someone to know

about today is that when I breathe, I breathe
real loud. Sometimes it's uncomfortable,

knowing the living are living. Very often, people
feel uneasy when we catch eyes in a room.

Sara Borjas

SAD BUT TRUE

She died watching *The Bachelorette* with Hot Cheeto fingers, the air conditioning left on, and the garbage full. Her neighbors complained she always let strangers in the apartment gate. What her sister remembers most is how she only used her blender twice and had mysterious bites on her shoulders. What her plants remember is how she had no discipline. What her brother remembers is how she didn't know shit. What the sink water remembers is how she didn't understand scope or range. What the door remembers is her bad posture and her lack of vision. What the mirror remembers is the flow it wanted to be. What her breath remembers is the empty frame of the door and men like they have just left through it. What her sister remembers is how she chased herself through the house, grasping the crispy air like a lover. She died with Hot Cheeto fingers. She died watching *The Bachelorette.*

Stephanie Adams-Santos

ZOPILOTE, ZOPILOTE

Zopilote, zopilote —
in your childhood ear
the word sounds like *sopa* & *elote,*
soup & corn — elements of a future-body

black soup, black corn
warm in the cazuela

You scavenge the things of memory:

bright red head of chile molido
crushed on the metate stone

lime, salt —

Roberto C. Garcia

#48124 [RECOVERED AUDIO SURVEILLANCE FILE | SOURCE: RECOVERED ORBITAL SURVEILLANCE SATELLITE]

dear prophet,

today i prayed about the ant. i prayed to make them away.
black boots. wave after wave. helmets. and guns.
like ants. carrying away mountains. scraps. skin.
i prayed about the ant. the ant. to make the soldiers good.
isn't that how it works, prophet? nobody taught me how.
the paper says it. the others. we argue. some kneel.
others do splits. others stand on their head.
one. the only old man in the whole world. neck wrapped in cloth.
body naked. prays nose to the wall. i prayed
from the good book. i prayed for the soldiers to be ants.
for the ants to be good.
i prayed to make them away.
nobody taught me how.

[recovered artifact #1,392,206 | source: religious text]

[6 Go to the ant consider wise!]
[it stores its food at harvest. 9 How long will you]
[A little sleep,]
[poverty will come on you like an armed man.]

[recovered artifact #1,398,400]

[pray Prophet saves us! Only the]
[Word in the Good Book]
[ ]
[end times!!!]

[catalogue and archive: class m planet: extinction level event]

[planet recoverable]

Christopher "Rooster" Martinez

LUNAR HALF-WAY PORT 78237

"We arrive where we must."
—Norma Elia Cantú

I'm tired of motherfuckers
thinking we left our barrios
back on Earth

aquí es la última frontera
y somos cosmic vatos!
generations eroded into the stars

even sin tierra madre—
sin Sur o Norte
darker & sunnier

pero frío como chingada!
all the homies came through—
Ramón, Suzi, Roy, Eva, all of 'em

It's still the "Westside"
even without "west"
even without San Antonio

between earth & moon
the contraband fireworks
still scare folks on both sides

of the divide
believing the sky is falling
or those Mexicans are having
too much fun

Christopher "Rooster" Martinez

NEPANTLA, USA CIRCA 3030

two boys are playing cops & robbers   one is dressed in Spanish
conquistador armor   the other   indigenous garb   everyday life occurs
around them   avoiding the battle   people shop   peruse
storefronts & vendors
the boy   (dressed for war) overtakes   the other   blood spills
in the form of flowers   & then   Spanish   & then   Mexico &
then   Texas   & then   U.S.   flags   a woman walks past
shrieking   as if   seeing   the violent ends   she leans
down   as if   to touch the boy   or raise soul   from soilinstead
pulls up a dollar   her face   registering the good luck   as if   the holograms
bleed   only in dreams

Raina J. León

BEYOND HARDWARE

i peruse paint samples to learn what shade names you. a blend of calumet cream and ivory and at your cheek blush rose, but i didn't need a color chart for that. at six months you have lost the shimmer that teens buy cheap or steal in their first transgressions. but for a time, there it was, free, this fleeting mica fleck, as if you were still dipped in celestial, all known and unknown elements you rode to my pulsing womb. all these months, i watched the stardust fade, the cosmic hold loosening to terra firma. and now, you are dressed in a soft blue onesie with little ears. what animal does capitalism say that you are? *your little one is safe and warm and held and ours,* it seems to say. stupid symbols, charts, and systems. stupid the act of reaching for a fixation. in my womb, i felt a girl and then at 10 weeks when your sex organs formed, a boy. now, sometimes i forget the sex i bore and use pronouns that are mine for you. shake loose of it all. i never asked you to tell me your name; you told me at your being's start. all i know is that i bore you. nursed you as i was able. only you can name you. i know nothing else.

Raina J. León

WISH PAINT

after "Superstition" by Luc Tuymans

oblivion fleshes out the shell
juts out in insect legs
or the jaggedness of drought fissures
its ear: a man's nipple
or a hoop earring caught in motion
at the other ear
it leaks tar streaks

behind the body
a man
bare and splayed
cut at chin, wrist and knee from view
all lines amputated
an ashy sheen that sharps
against the gallery's stark white

in black, I saw a wish baby
contorting from fly
a rough birthing
how we come into corporeal
color from thought

i turned y lo vi otra vez
sombra de sombra
el duende estira el lienzo
piel subiendo hueso

this is not the babe's laughter
after astral slide to tumble through a veil

this is the reason there are high
and locking gates

don't learn its name
it's already yours

Monique Quintana

MY SON'S ULTRASOUND BECOMES A VELVET PAINTING

His children build him a little house in the forest. Clown. There is no way to spy on the glow of cenote jelly, no way to count the rose clots that pass through the fresh to saltwater shore. They hear me weeping for my friend. I didn't let her give away the vegetables for free. My daughters will feed her plants in the open mouths of machines. My son, named after Juárez. Heed your mother's warnings. I lost the silver clippers, so I had to cut your nails with teeth. Your mother made your fingertip bright bluish for only a moment.

Monique Quintana

THE GRAMOPHONE

You found him near the sea, severed tentacles splayed on the rocks. He was all fish scales on his bottom half, mouth gunning with whiskey he took like medicine in another lifetime. Underneath the seafloor is our field of maíz, your ilium lined with a crown of fuse. He took a white woman as his lover in Chicago and gave her your gramophone. And the sea gave you permission to throw him back in the water.

Adriana M. Martínez Figueroa

MOUNTAIN WOMEN

I come from

mountain women

who've mastered their power.

Watch as they come down las curvas,

smelling del fogón,

a sheen of manteca on their foreheads,

strands of yuca still stuck to their teeth.

Watch as they shape me with chanclas

and banana leaves

y un calderito de arroz con pollo.

Watch as they scrape their burns off like pegao,

serve them to their husbands with a side of amarillos,

hardness with sweetness going down their loud throats with ease.

Watch as they level an entire cordillera with a single look.

Watch as they envelop you in their batas at night,

as they tell you about their days,

as they describe the skinny sato they fed outside work.

Watch as they revel in a love language stronger

than any gigante, dormido or not.

Watch as they cure you of ailments with

un sana sana,

un poquito de Vicks,

and the sound of a rosary's beads.

Watch.

You see that?

Tenderness turned power?

I'm dishing it out in the only way I know:

amorcito con sabor a recao.

Franchesca Lamarre

THIS COMPLEX BODY

They tell me I'm freedom.

Butt and body on fire.

They tell me to keep my feet up when the sun is down.

With my eyes closed, I look out of my window.

Over my left shoulder, I see an evergreen

full with leaves.

And they tell me its name means running Kalabash.

I like to think of myself as fruit with hot feet, always running somewhere new.

Naked and breathing

deep

with a heavy chest and careful hands.

Never available to hold all of what's to carry.

Now my lips are wet from sorrel made by our original hands,

and they too are never available to hold all of what's to carry.

I made up this room and all its smells.

So, we are left longing

to be let open

with loose sheets and running pillows turning cold on one side.

Turning cold on one side,

my back waits to feel the chill of the metal bar that situates

us.

This room begins with bed and ends at the wind of my ankle.

They tell me to keep my feet up when the sun is down.

They tell me I am patient with new pleasures that find me entangled, and these thighs

keep stretching for rescue.

I am sinking into myself.

They tell me to imagine my future.

They tell us to smile.

And I sit with shame: what is this love affair we have with punishment.
And I am left still.
And I am sitting here watching a black bird begin
to flutter its wings atop a brown fence,
wondering when she'll take flight.
Cause she is now surrounded by a still green but dying earth.
And they tell us to smile.
They tell me the beings I come from were the first to be freed.
They freed themselves
by setting fires.
Now take a look outside and inside cause we still here.
Still imaging futures
by setting fires.
They tell me I'm freedom.
They tell me I'm freedom.
They tell me I'm freedom.
Butt and body on fire.
They tell me to keep my feet up when the sun is down.
And it seems as though every time I am sat down by a failure, the floor beneath me
shifts my complacency.
And with every breath I let loose, an outpouring of champions must arrive.
Now, my lips are wet from guava nectar mixed with hand-poured waters.
And my bottom
still moist from hot sex just nine hours before.
Still oozing out the sentiments of pain, pleasure, and joy.
It's hard to imagine a woman's body without
those three.

They tell me I'm freedom.
They tell me I'm freedom.
They tell me I'm freedom.

The left strap to the white slip I am wearing seduces my back
just for the taste of my fingertips
to come hold us.
And my, are we soft.
And my, are we soft.

Beside me, a couplet of organic nature grows, and we're all letting out Queer smiles.

I am moved from my misting seat to water their brown vessels because their magic matters, too.
I am moved to drink an abundant amount of coconut water and write about

All of my magic.
All of my magic.
All of my magic.
Till my pen runs out of ink.
Their ink running down the brown bar of my arm,
Mama Audre calls it.
And now inked, we are moved toward Black futures.

We collect freedom.
We collect freedom.
We collect freedom.

Listening to my own voice, I hear her, us, and those before we.
To learn myself through them.
Aren't we always always in exchange?
And if I am held captive,
they tell me I already know what freedom is. And what it sounds like, feels like, tastes like, smells like.
Listen, cause we are always already imagining.
And when mama called and said I love you,
wasn't she kind?
Remember,
mamas just want to keep us safe. Black girls die to prove this.
Black mamas always throwing a lot of something into a pot.
Tea. Gumbo. Stew. Potion.
Themselves.
To heal us.
Black mamas don't know rest, not even after dinner comes.
They've made us their fruit.
They tell us to save the seeds.

I like to think of myself as fruit with hot feet, always running somewhere new.

They tell us to save the seeds.
They tell me I'm freedom
They tell us to smile.

We collect freedom.

Bailey Cohen

INAUGURATION DAY, 2021

after Kim Sousa

It is Wednesday. When did time become something
other than what the weather rules?

I watch the clock. I neglect the clouds.
I remember four years ago on this day

it rained,
and a fascist priest said it was a blessing

from God. A spiritual cleansing
for the president. Today, the winter sun dawned

the sky in a somehow-regular pink.
I've grown distrustful of Meaning.

Interpretation can be a weapon,
and I am a man who likes his sentences

sharp. I am newly militant
at the necessary rate.

I don't want reform. I want the total
abolition of the United States.

Bailey Cohen

THE SOLDIER IN THE CITY

A soldier walked toward the new city. Before he arrived, he admired the gold outlining all the
windows, the berries resting by the trees atop their roots. He lay down beneath a wide leaf's
shade. He grew tired, so he took a nap. When he woke, he walked into the city. There, a woman
on a bicycle rode by. Cars beeped exasperatingly at men on stubborn, immobile horses. Across
the street from the soldier, a woman turned a corner and acknowledged the cat on her front
porch. It was a beautiful day. The small creature flicked its tail. It looked at the soldier, then
tilted its head. Suddenly, the soldier felt extremely anxious. Who was he? Why was he here, in
this strange place? Did he know anything at all? His handsome children—his indelible
wife—had they been something he had loved and experienced, or was his existence beginning
now, at this very moment, within the cat's focused line of sight? Did the cat know about death? It
felt like death, the cat's held gaze. So the soldier began hesitantly to approach it, but the cat
straightened its posture, alert. In one swift leap as if rehearsed, it lunged at him and clawed at his
chest—but to the soldier, it felt like fists. It felt as if he was being pulled by plump gusts of wind.
He panicked, yelling, then ran into the street, the small animal still clinging to him, drawing
ceaselessly at his heart. The cars bellowed in disapproval. The horses raised their hooves in

distress. Eventually, dust filled the air, then settled. All the citizens approached the soldier's
bloodless body. Together, they said the city's oldest prayer. Then, the woman who had left the
cat on her porch came outside. The small creature climbed to her shoulders and rested there, like
berries atop branches. *You have known this is coming,* they said, to all who would listen. *Anyone*
who is able—arm yourselves. This soldier was the first and most innocent. His death was entirely
symbolic yet just as necessary as it was unfortunate. I almost wanted to tell him I was sorry it
had to be this way. Nevertheless, I will do what we must. I shall forget him, unless I die
tomorrow, in which case, I will think about him for the rest of my life.

Leila Ortiz

A POEM

a poem with images
a poem that tells a story
a poem with words omitted
a poem sitting at home
a poem skipping a stone across water
a poem with an attitude problem
a poem with a pain in its abdomen
a poem goes pee
a poem holds a spoon
a poem wishes wide open space
a poem coughs
a poem sings softly under its breath
a poem about death
a poem rains, it is raining
a poem wrapped in blankets
a poem makes the person cry
a poem is like that sometimes
a poem is hard to read
a poem tries to breathe
a poem misses her friends
a poem alone in a hospital bed
a poem is dying
a poem doesn't want to die
a poem pleads
a poem is a spell
a poem says fuck you
a poem doesn't know what to do
a poem tries to sm(eyes)
a poem is not my business
a poem is everyone's business

a poem grows a flower, the flower is yellow
a poem is a field of flowers
a poem is a field of flowers and a sky
a poem is a field of flowers and a sky and someone is dead
a poem with many dead
a poem in which it could have been avoided

Victoria Mallorga Hernandez

TWENTY YEARS UNDER THE BLACK TIDE

i stretch myself,
turn my hands toward the sleepless.
la vigilia que toma mi cuerpo cuando
las noticias repican a velocidad infinita.
against my eyes, the overwhelming beat
burning from within, anger braided into
my hair, waiting to remember bagua,
to remember helpless
& sleep to forget. to imbibe
another kind of dream where in rising,
alan garcia does not escape beyond death.
petroperu is charged & locked.
where the future builds into—
oil spills and massacres become
an old horror story your grandfather tells.
the generational trauma of a time before.
now that you have grown without it,
now that you don't have to hear the news extolling
the virtue of the *brave incredible* policías
que lucharon por sofocar la rebelión de
los nativos, porque claro,
que dirán los inversores
si los ciudadanos de segunda clase
se alzan una vez más.
but in this dreamfog, that's old history.
in the dreamfog,
estos ciudadanos de segunda clase have self-governed for years,
protecting the forest against the unbearable greed of transnational companies.
the amazonas running clear water for years, days mounting
a thousand trillion days since the last oil company's fuckup,
since the last time thoughts and prayers were offered instead of rescue,

years since the 500 oil spills in barely two decades, since the thousand
natives displaced, the marañón drowning darkside, the indifference crawling through
big cities
sitting in the softness of black gold.

in this dreamfog, oil no longer crosses the amazon,
communities heal, greenery grows reckless, growing
out of capitalist exploitation. the ground feeling
for once the shift of seasons without hunger.
and yet, memory remains, trauma hounding events
until they become a single repetitive nightmare.
la señorita bagua, tres nativos muertos,
delfines en crudo negro,
los derrames de petróleo crónicos e incalculables de la costa norte
details fading into dawn,

into my morning coffee,
anger beating on my hairline,
headlines screaming once more the same story:
oil spills across the river line.

Note: In 2009, President Alan Garcia said the Indigenous protestors in Bagua were not "ciudadanos de primera clase" (first class citizens), insinuating that they were not fully-fledged citizens and had no right to make decisions over their lands (https://www.youtube.com/watch?v=yjzxl1lBswc).
This happened during el Baguazo, where indigenous leaders protested clauses in the Trade Promotion Agreement between Peru and the United States that would open their territory to exploitation by transnational companies, a decision that had been taken unilaterally by the Peruvian state.

Leslie Sainz

WILL THE LAST AMERICAN TO LEAVE MIAMI PLEASE BRING THE FLAG?

Roaches on the ceiling—even they don't want to walk
where we walk

Dead brain
twitch
begging for it

NPR says the city has rented refrigerated container trucks
to store the overflow of bodies.

The officer asks to see our legs
in the air, a struggle.

When something of mine breaks
or we bruise from impact—

That's G-d.

Leslie Sainz

THREAT DISPLAY

"Exploding a few plastic bombs in carefully chosen spots, the arrest of Cuban agents and the release of prepared documents substantiating Cuban involvement also would be helpful in projecting the idea of an irresponsible government."

—"Justification for US Military Intervention in Cuba (TS)," Washington, DC, 13 March, 1962.

Unfastening
the smallest bones

of the rebellion.

Auditory snow:

        A kick to the head
that misses.

(*Sana, sana, colita de rana*)

Does the spic cover
their ears long after?

*

Blood woofer.

Counterintelligent.

A specter
in the vestibule—

Bolshevik?—

A check
of the exits.

*

In utero,
the ear develops

on the lower neck
before moving

upward.

More scraping
of the sides,

more sliding.

*

You could fit
a brain

in a bass drum,
a snare drum,

a floor tom.

You could
hold it

up like a boom.

P.L. Sanchez

BARRIO DE HIGUERETA

At the military school where my parents once threatened to enroll me,
they always play the Peruvian national anthem. The first two words
are somos libres. We are free. At my apartment a block away,
I can hear them. It's like a story tailored for us. We picture our liberator
José de San Martín charging into a platoon of Spanish soldiers.
Then, the trombone plays the wrong note. It throws them off balance.
Before they start over, the teachers have a cigarette break outside.
When my father was fourteen, his own father split a guitar open on his head.
He tells me a different version of the story each time.
I've heard of him skipping school for weeks and smoking weed in a shallow pool.
I see his face in the trombone player leaving the school. When he gets home,
his mother hands him a gun. Father is at the movies with another woman.
Years later, a couple moves into my old apartment. They are unhappy,
or so the neighbor tells me. The woman works until morning, and the man
takes a third of her paycheck for himself. Her family packs up his bags
when he's not around, but he builds a trench out of wool and cotton,
hiding behind the front lines. *I won't come out,* he says.
When the neighbor finishes his story, I pick up the tab.
One more for the road, he says, his feet telling two separate parables.
One taps, the other one trembles.

Jose Hernandez Diaz

THE SHOWDOWN

A man in a Rage Against the Machine shirt overthrew the government—of his house. Moreover, he successfully defeated his wife and three-year-old daughter in an argument about what to watch on television. The wife and child wanted to watch *Frozen* for the 77th time. The Man in a Rage Against the Machine shirt wanted to watch the Dodger game.

They decided to play rock, paper, scissors. The man faced his child. He drew rock. She drew scissors. The man jumped up and down. *Victory! Sweet victory,* he shouted. When the Dodger game was over, the man swept the kitchen, mopped, and threw out the trash. His wife and child had fallen asleep thirty minutes earlier watching Elsa do princess things.

Sara Borjas

DINNER TABLE SONNET

If I ask my father to speak to me and my brother
tells me to be quiet, is this critique? If I assess

the absence of reason in his request as a pattern,
is this theory? Is it experimental to ask your dad

to speak to you while eating dinner, and technique
when your brother says to *shhh*? Is this, perhaps,

historical approach? If I evaluate the details by which
I am being anti-evaluated, is this meta? paratextual?

manipulative? Once, my therapist asked me how I felt
about what I asked for. Once, my professor asked me

how I felt about how I felt about everything. Once,
I told my father how I felt about how I felt about

him never talking to me. My father sighed, exhausted,
and ate a potato. I can't tell if men love me.

Sara Borjas

POEM I IMAGINE MY MOTHER WOULD WRITE TO ME

Mija, you'd make a good mom. You hate everything
I hate. I am sorry for giving you that. You teach me to be proud

of myself with words I know. I'm afraid you'll never love
anyone more than me, that maybe I wounded you

with all the unclaimed love I never had from my mother.
When she looked me in the face, her hand followed out

from the hole your grandpa left in her. We are just trying
to find an end now. I don't know if all this opening

is the right way. You say things meaning well, but aren't good
at being outside of you. I am afraid you'll hurt someone

when you try to love them and they don't know
about us. I know I drink too much, but I'm afraid

of what's inside my life. I am not as brave as you is what
I tell myself but maybe the thing is more terrible than you

can ever imagine. I feel bad for everyone but myself.
That's why I married your dad. I am glad you don't have

that weighing you down. I got it for us both and I like carrying
us, too. That's what God is I think sometimes, the carrier

of all the stone and rock our lives break into. I don't talk
about God much because I don't feel smart enough

to speak about it but I know that you want me to change.
I want to change too. I don't know who I am, mija,

other than you and your brother and sister. I don't know
who I am without you, and I'm scared. When you

gave me the poem about grandma slapping me, I felt
real. And I felt proud, even though it hurt.

Sara Borjas

I AM A SIXTH SUN XICANA FROM PINEDALE

after Mia Barraza's "i am a sixth sun xicana"

I am a sixth sun xicana
with a farmworker's twang and a lowrider's frame
tree trunk hips and salt split lips
I've got solar-soaked skin a donkey's grin
my mother's wooden bones
and my father's vast wounds
eucalyptus for feet and knees plump
as oranges and my hair straight as grass
along a dry dirt ditch

I've worn yoga pants to a ball
and beer for a personality
I've paid for pleasure with my dignity
and chosen propriety over my mom's cooking
I've marched for women and stood
with double-faced goose-steppers
I've won acceptance with lies
and painted my nails with sink water

I don't tell others they have it easy
I don't forgive killer cops or war criminals or racists
I don't feed others before myself or wonder
if I should have said something
I speak my mind to the hierarchs
I make jokes with my heart
I argue with the work trucks
and the belt buckles that convince
people they must be men

I ride low in my shame & my pride
I leave the doubtful in a neon dust
I don't forget the dead or the devastated
or history's hidden trails
I record the valley
I dress up in tight ego
I peek through the berserk to see
what's likely tomorrow
I spot women tight as a bunch of grapes sweeping
their minds into a 14k plated monument
with one amused, bizarre soul,
infinite crop rows for legs

Alessandra Nysether-Santos

LEGACY

I am bound to this tree.
You see, my heart inherited
my ancestors, and so, each day,
my heart is picked clean.

The women in my family pass down
ever-heavier hearts, heirlooms
doomed to be broken over and over.
Cracked cup pouring into cracked cup
pouring into cracked cup, chipping
one another with cheers turned clatter.

Shattering each other with fists and tongue-whips,
clipping the wings of their young
to protect them from the fall, pushing them out
to protect them from being *too soft*.

Inherited trauma
does not make my destiny.

Abuse is not a birthright—
it is a legacy.

A tradition carried out like execution,
a heaviness you cannot bear.
All these eyes turned away,
that unbearable loneliness,
what I fear:

a whole life unseen.
Providing, providing, providing.
A whole life unseeing.
Abiding, abiding, abiding.

A heart picked clean
unless you guard it.

Lock it, like your mother's.

Vincent Toro

CINEPHRASTIC: SLEEP DEALER (DIR. ALEX RIVERA, 2009)

Dry, this mesa. What is potable siphoned
by droneshepherds warding these hinter
lands. Their lenses sniff me hyperpoaching
company waves. Delete my source code,
spurring migration via system integration.
My rural gone obsolete. Bail to cop work

as dermal conduit. Repurposed by coyote tech. Ahora soy
prosthetic stoop labor. Discarnate appendages uprooting

cassava via live stream. The innovation
this demesne of capital gain has sought:
an interface that unBrowns the goods.
Each hour spent betahitched to network
of cyber-maquilas surges my amaurosis.
Neural bandwidth atrophies when chains

go asomatous. Mi memoria outsourced to depleted
sectors, embezzled and greased to snooze pilferers.

Nodehunted. Ramsacked. My narco
processors watt sapped, until Luz hemo
hacks wetware syncretism. Until meta
carpal of droneshepherds hits ctrl-alt
del. Hops mode and margin. Excises
ill logic gate that robohews granjero

from extranjero. Inducing bit torrent deluge of ancient
rain to el campo. Leveejack. Bolt for new motherboard.

previously published in *Tertulia* (Penguin Random House, 2020)

Stephanie Adams-Santos

ZACULEU OF TOMORROW, ZACULEU OF YESTERDAY

At the first altar of blood
there was hardly a sound
but a trembling, something in the earth.
a murmuring of teeth and mycelia,
simple cries—
ayyy ayyy

sounds moving like slugs in the grass
of the body, leaving their traces of memory,
the slow sound of the earth digesting.

This is what you must listen for.
The sounds that spill from the hands
and burrow deep into earth,
thickening in syrups, growing old and silent.
Fossils do not only live in stone.

Stephanie Adams-Santos

TOTAL MEMORY

A small man in the jungle of Tikal
blesses himself with leopard's dung

In the shade of an achiote shrub
he makes his cheeks red,

under your pillow, he leaves a mirror
a slab of black stone
while you dream

an opening that never closes

where the old women of your head
walk in procession,

endlessly coming
and going

Aerik Francis

ARS POETICA GENERATIONXXX

Denver, Colorado, USA 2019 CE

after Joseph Rios's "Ars Poetica, Three Generations"

"So you are dying in their etymology"[1]

We vestiges of
his stories of
sexuality[2]

Scientia Sexualis *Ars Erotica*

Ago a wight French masc came
to Mexico already invaded by Spain
He met a particular darker femme

it was fatal attraction
it was natal alienation[3]

generations later
it was Me

Ago a wight English masc came
to Xaymaca already invaded by Spain
He met a particular darker femme

[1] From "Verso 15.1" in *The Blue Clerk* by Dionne Brand
[2] "An entire glittering sexual array, reflected in a myriad of discourses, the obstination of powers, and the interplay of knowledge and pleasure." From *History of Sexuality* by Michel Foucault
[3] "... the term 'natal alienation' ... goes directly to the heart of what is critical in the slave's forced alienation, the loss of ties of birth in both ascending and descending generations." From *Slavery and Social Death* by Orlando Patterson

it was fatal
it was natal
generations
it was
gene   rations

it was
Me

it was
later
my
name

Etymology *Genealogy*
Tragoedia *Comoedia*

LatinXXX

Aerik Francis

STASIS: WAITING 4 FRANK OCEAN

They are waiting. Keep them waiting. Make people wait.

∞

I waited here for you / I knew you no saint / I accepted your wait / The weight is one I'm acquainted with / I think you've seen the dark too / Heard a bang / another plane place and space rearranged / *in the dark* / I heard more than I felt than I saw / I heard swirls and gusts in my gut/ I heard drums and rumblings in my heart / they played Indefinitely / Sun lost its supremacy / I witnessed it with ebon pupils / Hours / our Hours proxies an approximation amalgamation abomination objective subjugation / It just ain't feel right / It couldn't describe the Time / it took for the air to enter / our chests and sink heavily in our bodies dark / It couldn't describe the darkness / the pit on the map / where our ancestors laughed / Millennia ago such that their voices forever linger on the lips of these moving shadows /

Time is / Music is / I shower / to two Songs / run to six / cry to one, two, more and more these ||: Days / Weeks / Months / Rewind Repeat :|| What do heart beats sound like / in the hold of ships / Wretched infernal polyphonic pounding / pulsing booms of energy / We embrace long enough for our beats to sync / Imagine / a measure of a humxn / in sanguine aorta applause /

Sometimes the consequences are much better than the anxiety before the judgment / Uncertainty / Waiting in the row – crossing off ||: Days / Weeks / Years :|| working until the royal guillotine drops / Nothing new under the Sun / but the end of the solar system is not the end / of the universe ||: Centuries / Millennia :|| and the Sun implodes again in perfect icy black /

And yet the uncanny ability to blink and render each of these Futures as moot / in the warm silence of the Present / and that itchy urge for pleasure / seems nice for Now / I'm not as courageous as I / Imagine myself to be / I find myself traveling with the weather / yet and still discovering myself / mucking in dim swamps, in sticky quagmires / downfall drifting in the undertow of the backwater / *In the dark* / of the Day

∞

And I'm weighting, and you're waiting.

Michelle Moncayo

DANCE LESSONS

My holographic cacti   leather femmes in green
their spines teach me to stand upright

I drag   my robes of tulle   glide in the smoke of them

The sun unbuttons me
my hips are Caribe
I dance to Fania in pasties

the stars recognize my tits
they tip their top hats down to me
eat my pink canned femme my neon floral
bless me with a tweed suit and the spine of a tiger
drag the stubble out of my body

the singers in orange   their hair of static   they slip the harness around me
I am a tiger   eating the camera
my orange tits skip   I am the cherry of the lights
then a swatch of paint   talking to Basquiat

Chavela Vargas sings from beneath the clouds
ponme la mano aquí macorina
Josephine Baker teaches me how to kiss with my eyes

I am the spine of a candle
standing upright   singing in orange

then out in a
(kind of) blue

Michelle Moncayo

PROVERBS FROM A QUEER BURLESQUE DANCER

1:1

May the vergüenza turn into tassels.

Pop the hip.
Cock the eyebrow.
Twirl the tassels.
Your tits are the stars themselves, winking.

Do you see the light your body casts in the dark?
The way you become the solar flares when you dance?
How you can sequin yourself back into life?

1:2

May you learn to untie the corset off your tongue
and let your Spanish shimmy open doors.

Tu voz es un aguacero
de cacao en el campo,
un merengue en el colmado,

Abuela's accent & her Abuela's accent,
y todos que vinieron antes.

Que acento mas bello
they would tell you
no matter how you speak or don't speak.

Your voice is a handwritten letter,
the blessing of your ancestors.

1:3
May you always reach for the fine silverware
and the fancy plates you reserve for your husband and visitas
and serve yourself all the good plátanos first.

Let your husband serve his own plate.
You do not owe him your body, your labor, or anything else,
and there are only so many mouths to feed in a lifetime.

So use the fine silverware,
dress in your favorite silk robe,
and serve yourself first.

1:4
In this house, the house of Sin Vergüenza,
we all have a future.
We can runway our bodies,
fluid and expansive like the ocean,
into a life that is ours.

There are no gods that will set fire to our feet
or denounce us for stripping into what we are.
Here, queer is a word we say in Spanish and in English.

We are always   enough
and never have to quantify ourselves to anyone.

Here, we dance whenever we want to
wear whatever we want to
strip whenever we want to.

What land would call this, us, sin?
We are a blessing, undressed.

Michelle Moncayo

HERE, ON THIS 76L BUS

at the corner of Belgrove & Woodland,
women like Ma and Abuelita get on
fumbling change, child in hand.

Their heads: a garden of plastic rolos
yellow, red, green, curls waiting to sprout.
The garden: good luck & each rolo: a wish.

Pa' que no se vaya la luz
Pa' que llueva café en el campo
Pa' que mis hijos tengan lo que no tuve yo
Pa' que siempre haya comida y familia

We pass the fish market with the white letters
thin & outstretched like the spine of bacalao.

Next stop: American Steel Strip, 900 Passaic Ave.
The factory where Abuelita worked making pencils
those first years in the States. Vines climb
up the sides of the browned building.

On Broad Street & 8th, you can still buy calling cards.

Next stop & more climb on:
a little girl with trenzas down her back & a purple romper,
Mami's hand in one hand, a muñeca in the other.

Every morning, the congregation on the bus speaks.

Y de donde eres?

Soy Dominicana, but they say I don't sound it (whatever that means).
Soy Ecuatoriana, but they say I don't sound it (whatever that means).

Mixed Ma's Spanish with Pa's Spanish & the needle on my tongue skips.

I've never been back home, *but I know the sound of home.*
It's been years since I've been back, *but I'm saving to go home.*

Trabajo en la bodega *en la escuela* *I'm working on my career*

At the salon *law school* *cytology* *homeless shelter*

This bus is just another stop *on the way.*
I get on the bus y me dicen,
Que dios te bendiga.

& I don't know about Dios or if the church would want me, but
Que dios te bendiga & I'm at the bodega below Abuelita's house
& we got all the good plátanos today and the culebritas for free y

Que dios te bendiga and Ma finished up her degree y

Que dios te bendiga & I can see that they see me
y me invitan a comer habichuela con dulce y

Que dios te bendiga
& Juan Luis Guerra is singing & it's a backyard party
& there's enough Presidentes to go around y

Que dios te bendiga & we won the lotería
& the rain finally came
& the guava trees are in full bloom
& we make it to the last stop home.

Michelle Moncayo

A POTION FOR CURING DEPRESSION

Wait until the full moon is out on a summer night. This is when the nimitas come out—the ancestors, those who have passed on. Their light will guide you to the proper body of water.

Dress in a slip, tie a pañuelo around your curls the way Mami taught you. Walk barefoot as she did. Kneel down and press your palms to the earth. Feel the dirt on your hands, let it read the fortune lines on your palm. Tonight, the earth needs to know you. It too has held what you hold.

When you get to the river, take out the lightboxes you use for the depression. Unscrew the bulbs, then crush them into a fine dust. Sprinkle them into the caldo first.

Take out the clear jars, the ones filled with your friends' laughter, that you let marinate for seven days under the full moon. Spoon them into the caldo. Listen to the way they run through the trees when released.

Take out the coconut oil and smooth it over your skin and hair. Spoon the rest into the caldo. Add salt.

Steep six leaves of guayusa in river water. Let the moonlight sink into the leaves.

Listen for the voices of the ancestors. Ask them to speak their cures into the leaves. Place them in the caldo. Add the water of the river. Bring to a boil.

Watch the way the nimitas gather over the caldo. Open your palms to the smoking potion. Lean your bones into it. Imagine it is the healing hands of those who have passed through it, too.

Franchesca Lamarre

BLACK TO THE FUTURE

Free for the individual,

healing for the community.

Born

into a world.

One that made space

for

uncentered forms.

Bright eyes

rest

from

pollination.

A cycle of

comfortable surviving.

We seek broken language, laughter,

and

pause

at liberation.

Not my Freedom.

Not my kingdom.

Soon to forget

where we've been.

Drugged and dancing

to the drum.

One we created.

To love.

To live.

To lift.

Transform.

Spirits and time in motion.

Movement.

Trauma is shifting.

Jolt out
and cry

a river.

Drink the medicine.

Emerge FREE.

Only, you've left the
bottle open.

Behind you,
a sibling cries
and pours out

his laughter.

Looks through you
to see

himself centered.

With shoulders fixed to stand tall,

unwind your back to lunge and parallel yourself

uncomfortable.

We seek their story.

Come and be let

out.

Into winds you'll wake.

Whistle when you see us falling.
Whistle when you see us still.

Make noise for our vibrations.

Resound resilience.

Remember.

Free for the the individual,

Healing for the community.

Intersect and storm.

Punch clouds and shake the rain free.

You taste earth.
You are water.
You wear wind.

Let fire be mine.

I told you when I was coming,
brought you back to sow new homes.

I will burn the grounds
before you strip me of them.

Wakiena Remembers!

Sweet canes.
Dry rot.

Don't lie.
Don't dance for foolery.
Don't drink to holler.
Don't die to dream.
We are the weapon of truth.

Our bodies cannot be bought.
Coins cannot bring us fruit.
We share space.
Know time.
And be.
Intelligent.

Circles of freedom. Stored practice.

Orisha.
Oracle.
Open,

self to listen.
Vomit your truth
Wrap up in cleansed leaves.

Bury you.
Re-emerge
Free for the individual,

Healing for the community.

Deconstruct

your Blackened
mind.

Feed it.
Hot wax.
Cool stones.
Loud flowers.

Dark rum.
Deep and dirty rice.
Hot waters in corn-fielded ovens.

Sticky wings,
washed down
with watermelons.

We are the
empty spaces
filling voids
of

stiff language.

And it's
too discerning. Of mine,

I speak
zero bionic

ebonics.

Unwritten free notes.
Don't taunt us
with

your

malleable tongue.

My
Drum won't

cum

to your arrangements.

We be
spoken language
destinations

without
patience.

Our room.
Our room.
Our room.

Entry stipulations.

You can't say it.
You can't weigh it.
You ain't paid it.

Remember,
Free for the individual,

Healing for the community.

C. T. Salazar

PRAYER IN REVERSE

zero in / o divisible crosshair
YHWH says I am that I am, so too
x would say / if it had a mouth
when the gun has two barrels
vote for less bullets / vote for
utopia or whatever place you
think we can live peacefully /
string these lights up—*do this in*
remembrance of me, he said and
quietly, they obliged / isn't it wild
push a phone and it rings down the cliff / I
opened my jacket at the checkpoint
no sir, I said / *I'm just trying get home*
my mother is already reciting her scriptures
look how the cemetery is already
kicking itself loose / to make more room
just when I was believing
I could deadbolt my door / door my indigo away

:::

hold me like June's our
god-given fruit / our farewell to
famine, hold me—I heard the riot's
ending / I heard we got what we
dreamed / how jubilant, to
celebrate with you if only
briefly pretending / this land is ours—
america, my hands are raised /
you can see them

Biographical Information

Kim Sousa (they/she) is a queer Brazilian American poet, editor, and open border radical. She was born in Goiânia, Goiás, and immigrated to Austin, Texas, with her family at age five. Her poems can be found in *Poet Lore, EcoTheo Review, The Boiler, Missouri Review, [PANK]* Magazine's Latinx Lit Celebration, Harvard's *PALABRITAS,* and elsewhere. Her debut poetry collection, *ALWAYS A RELIC NEVER A RELIQUARY,* is the winner of the Black Lawrence Press 2020 St. Lawrence First Book Prize and is forthcoming July 2022. Along with *Até Mais,* she is the co-editor of the limited-run anthology of immigrant and first-generation poetry, *No Tender Fences,* which donated 100% of its proceeds to the immigrant advocacy network RAICES Texas. You can find Kim at Twitter @kimsoandso and @LatinxFuturisms.

Malcolm Friend (he/him) is a poet originally from the Rainier Beach neighborhood of Seattle, Washington. He received his BA from Vanderbilt University and his MFA from the University of Pittsburgh. He is the author of the chapbook *mxd kd mixtape* (Glass Poetry, 2017) and the full-length collection *Our Bruises Kept Singing Purple* (Inlandia Books, 2018), winner of the 2017 Hillary Gravendyk Prize. Together with JR Mahung, he is a member of Black Plantains, an Afrocaribbean poetry collective. He currently lives and teaches high school in Austin, TX.

Alan Chazaro is the author of *This Is Not a Frank Ocean Cover Album* (Black Lawrence Press, 2019), *Piñata Theory* (Black Lawrence Press, 2020), and *Notes from the Eastern Span of the Bay Bridge* (Ghost City Press, 2021). He is a graduate of June Jordan's Poetry for the People program at UC Berkeley and a former Lawrence Ferlinghetti Poetry Fellow at the University of San Francisco. Raised in the San Francisco Bay Area by Mexican immigrants, he's currently an arts reporter at *KQED*. His work can be found in *GQ, LA Times, SLAM, Believer Magazine* and more.

J.C. Rodriguez (he/siya) is a Filipino-Peruvian writer from Westbury, NY. His poems have appeared in places such as *Brooklyn Poets, Waxwing,* and *Meow Meow Pow Pow.* He is a manuscript reader at Interstellar Flight Press.

Christopher "Rooster" Martinez is an educator and spoken word poet from San Antonio, Texas. He earned a MA/MFA in Creative Writing, Literature & Social Justice at Our Lady of the Lake University. He is the author of two poetry books: *A Saint for Lost Things* (Alabrava Press, 2020) and *As it is in Heaven* (Kissing Dynamite Poetry Press, 2020).

Vincent Toro is a Boricua poet, playwright, and professor. He is the author of three poetry collections: *Hivestruck* (Penguin Random House, 2024), *Tertulia* (Penguin Random House, 2020) and *Stereo.Island.Mosaic.* (Ahsahta, 2016), which won the Poetry Society of America's Norma Farber First Book Award. Vincent is a recipient of the Caribbean Writer's Cecile De Jongh Poetry Prize, the Spanish Repertory Theater's Nuestras Voces Playwriting Award, a Poet's House Emerging Poets Fellowship, a New York Council for the Arts Fellowship in Poetry, and a New Jersey State Council for the Arts Writer's Fellowship. His poetry and prose have been published in dozens of magazines and journals and has been anthologized in Saul Williams's *CHORUS, Puerto Rico En Mi Corazon, Best American Experimental Writing 2015, Misrepresented People,* and T*he Breakbeat Poets Vol. 4: LatiNEXT*. He is an Assistant Professor of English at Rider University, is a Dodge Foundation Poet, and is a contributing editor for Kweli Literary Journal.

Joel Salcido was born in the San Fernando Valley and raised in West Phoenix. He is the son of Mexican immigrants, a first-generation college graduate, a husband, & father of three sons. Joel is a graduate of the MFA program at Arizona State University.

Born in Puerto Rico, **Tatiana Figueroa Ramirez** graduated with a B.A. in English Literature, holds a master's in Public Management with a focus on Nonprofit Management and Leadership, and is a VONA Voices alumna, having worked with Willie Perdomo and Danez Smith. Tatiana currently performs, facilitates workshops, and hosts events in the DC area, having previously done so across the United States and the Dominican Republic at venues including New York University and The Kennedy Center. Much of her community and poetic efforts are dedicated to amplifying marginalized voices and empowering young women of color. You can read her work in the *Acentos Review*, among other publications. Tatiana is the author of *Coconut Curls y Café con Leche* (2019) and *Despojo* (2020).

SG Huerta is a queer Xicanx writer from Dallas. They are the poetry editor of Abode Press and marketing co-director for *Split Lip Magazine*. SG is the author of two poetry chapbooks, *The Things We Bring with Us* (Headmistress Press, 2021) and *Last Stop*

(Defunkt Magazine, 2023), and the nonfiction chapbook *GOOD GRIEF* (fifth wheel press, 2025). A Roots Wounds Words Fellow and Tin House Alum, their work has appeared in *Barrelhouse, Honey Literary, Bodega Magazine, The Offing, Infrarrealista Review,* and elsewhere. Find them at sghuertawriting.com, or in Texas with their partner and two cats.

Dimitri Reyes is a Puerto Rican multidisciplinary teaching artist, content creator, and writer from Newark, New Jersey. He has been named one of The Best New Latinx Authors of 2023 by LatinoStories.com for his most recent book, *Papi Pichón* (Get Fresh Books, 2023), which was a finalist for the Omnidawn chapbook contest and the Andrés Montoya Poetry Prize. His other books include *Every First and Fifteenth,* the winner of the Digging Press 2020 Chapbook Award, and the poetry journal *Shadow Work for Poets,* now available on Amazon. Dimitri's work has been nominated for a Pushcart Prize and Best of the Net and you can find more of his writing in Poem-a-Day, *Vinyl, Kweli,* and *Acentos.* In 2023, he was also part of the inaugural poetry cohort for the Poets & Writers Get The Word Out publishing incubator. Currently, he is a 2024 NJ Arts Professional Learning Institute (APLI) fellow. Dimitri is also the Marketing & Communications Director at CavanKerry Press.

Leo Boix is a bilingual Latinx poet born in Argentina who lives and works in the UK. His debut English collection, *Ballad of a Happy Immigrant* (Chatto & Windus, 2021), was awarded the PBS Wild Card Choice and was selected as one of the best five books of poetry by the *Guardian* (August 2021). He has authored another two books, in Spanish, *Un Lugar Propio* (2015) and *Mar de Noche* (2017), both with Letras del Sur Editora, Argentina. His book *To Love a Woman* (Poetry Translation Centre-PTC, 2022), a collection of poems by the Argentine queer writer Diana Bellesi, received a PEN Translate Prize. Boix has been included in many anthologies, such as *Ten: Poets of the New Generation* (Bloodaxe), *The Best New British and Irish Poets Anthology 2019-2020* (BlackSpring Press), *Islands Are But Mountains: Contemporary Poetry from Great Britain* (Platypus Press), *100 Poems to Save the Earth* (Seren Books), *Why I Write Poetry* (Nine Arches Press), and *Un Nuevo Sol: British Latinx Writers* (flipped eye), among others. His poems have appeared in many national and international journals, including *POETRY, PN Review,* the *Poetry Review, Modern Poetry in Translation,* the *Manchester Review,* the *White Review, Ambit,* the *London Magazine, Asymptote,* the *Morning Star,* the *Rialto, Magma Poetry, Letras Libres, Litro Magazine, BathMag, Prism International, Contra journal,* the *Acentos Review,* and elsewhere. Boix is a fellow of The Complete Works program, co-director of Un Nuevo Sol, an Arts Council national scheme to nurture new voices of Latinx writers in the UK, and an advisory board member of the Poetry Translation Centre. He has written poems commissioned by Royal Kew Gardens, the National Poetry Library, Bradford Literary Festival, Un Nuevo Sol and La Linea Festival, among others. Boix is also a mentor for the Ledbury Poetry Critics scheme run by the University of Liverpool and for the Jerwood Compton Poetry Fellowships scheme. He was the recipient of the Bart Wolffe Poetry Prize Award 2018 and the Keats-Shelley Prize 2019, as well as being awarded The Charles Causley International Poetry Competition 2021 (2nd prize).

Aline Mello is a Brazilian immigrant raised in the South. She is the author of *More Salt than Diamond* (Andrews McMeel, 2022), her first poetry collection. Her work has been twice nominated for a Pushcart Prize and has been included in anthologies such as *Breakbeat Poets: Latinext* and *Somewhere We Are Human*. Her poems have been published in journals that include the *New Republic*, Poets.org's Poem-A-Day, the *Georgia Review*, and others. She is an Undocupoet fellow and has an MFA in creative writing from The Ohio State University.

Lysz Flo is an AfroCaribbean Latine, polyglot (Haitian Creole, Spanish, French), spoken word artist, educator, and indie author, member of The Estuary Collective, *Creatively Exposed* podcast host, Voodoonauts Summer 2020 Fellow and Obsidian Black Listening 2022 Fellow. She released her poetry novel *Soliloquy of an Ice Queen*, March 2020. Her poems can be found in *Royal Rose Mag, Hellebore, Skin Coloured Mag*, and Digging Press and she has done various multimedium project work for O' Miami. Creative writing workshops holder at GrubStreet. Online Crystal and Spiritual wellness shop owner at Astrolyszics.com.

Gustavo Barahona-López is a writer and educator from Richmond, California. In his writing, Barahona-López draws from his experience growing up as the son of Mexican immigrants. His micro-chapbook *Where Will the Children Play?* was part of the Ghost City Press 2020 Summer Series. He was a finalist for the 2021 Quarterly West poetry prize and his chapbook *Loss and Other Rivers That Devour* was published in February 2022 by Nomadic Press. A member of the Writer's Grotto and a VONA alum, Barahona-López's work can be found or is forthcoming in *Iron Horse Literary Review, Puerto del Sol*, the *Acentos Review, Apogee Journal*, and *Hayden's Ferry Review*, among other publications.

Aerik Francis is a Queer Black & Latinx poet born & based in Denver, Colorado, USA. Aerik is the recipient of poetry fellowships from CantoMundo and The Watering Hole. Aerik is also the recipient of the Amiri Baraka Scholarship for Naropa

University's 2019 Summer Writing Program and the Robert Hayden Scholarship for Stockton University's 2021 Winter Poetry & Prose Getaway. Aerik is a poetry reader for Underblong poetry journal and is event coordinator for Slam Nuba. With poetry published widely in print and on the net, find out more about their work at phaentompoet.com or via social media @phaentompoet.

Anthony Cody is the author of *Borderland Apocrypha* (Omnidawn, 2020) and *The Rendering* (Omnidawn, 2023). He has been recognized as a winner of a 2021 American Book Award and a 2020 Southwest Book Award, as well as a finalist for the National Book Award, PEN America / Jean Stein Award, L.A. Times Book Award, and the California Book Award. Anthony is a Poets & Writers 2020 Debut Poet. His poetry has appeared in the *Academy of American Poets: Poem-A-Day Series, Gulf Coast, Ninth Letter, Prairie Schooner, TriQuarterly, The Boiler, ctrl+v journal,* the *Colorado Review,* and *MAGMA Poetry* (UK), among others. He is a CantoMundo fellow from Fresno, CA, with lineage in the Bracero Program and Dust Bowl. Anthony is co-publisher of Noemi Press, an editor at Omnidawn, a collaborator with Juan Felipe Herrera and the Laureate Lab Visual Wordist Studio, and is faculty in poetry at Randolph College's Low Residency MFA Program.

Darrel Alejandro Holnes is an Afro-Panamanian American writer. His plays have received productions or readings at the Kennedy Center for the Arts American College Theater Festival (KCACTF), The Brick Theater, Kitchen Theater Company, Pregones Theater/PRTT, Primary Stages, and elsewhere. He is a member of the Lincoln Center Director's Lab, Civilians R&D Group, Page 73's Interstate 73 Writers Workshop, and other groups. His play *Starry Night* was a finalist for the Eugene O'Neill Theater Center's National Playwrights Conference and the Princess Grace Award in Playwriting. His play *Bayano* was also a finalist for the Eugene O'Neill Theater Center's National Playwrights Conference. His most recent play, *Black Feminist Video Game,* was produced by The Civilians for 59E59, Oregon Shakespeare Festival, Center Theater Group, and other theaters and venues and won an inaugural Anthem Award. He is the founder of the Greater Good Commission and Festival, a festival of Latinx short plays. Holnes is the author of *Migrant Psalms* (Northwestern University Press, 2021) and *Stepmotherland* (Notre Dame Press, 2022). He is the recipient of the Andres Montoya Poetry Prize from Letras Latinas, the Drinking Gourd Poetry Prize, and a National Endowment for the Arts Literature Fellowship in Creative Writing (Poetry). His poem "Praise Song for My Mutilated World" won the C. P. Cavafy Poetry Prize from Poetry International. He is an assistant professor of English at Medgar Evers College, a senior college of the City University of New York

(CUNY), and a faculty member at New York University. For more information visit www.darrelholnes.com.

Yania Padilla Sierra is an Afro-Boricua poet, writer, and suicide prevention SME. She is a Cantomundo fellow and Associate Editor at *Frontier*. Her poetry and essays have been published in various literary journals including *Bacopa Literary Review* and *River River*.

Newark, NJ native **Ysabel Y. González**, received her BA from Rutgers University and an MFA in Poetry from Drew University. Ysabel has received invitations to attend VONA, Tin House, CantoMundo and BOAAT Press workshops. In her work, Ysabel explores her neurodivergence, Borinquen roots, and how to engage with tenderness in a complicated world. She is a Pushcart Prize nominee and the author of *Wild Invocations* (Get Fresh Books, 2019). You can find her in New Jersey living with her husband and two furbabies, crafting, tending to her garden, and reading tarot. Visit www.ysabelgonzalez.com for more.

Ruben Reyes Jr. is the son of Salvadoran immigrants and the author of the story collection, *There is a Rio Grande in Heaven*. He is a graduate of the Iowa Writers' Workshop and Harvard College. His writing has appeared in the *Boston Globe*, the *Washington Post*, *Lightspeed Magazine*, and other publications. Originally from Southern California, he now lives in Brooklyn.

Steve Castro is a Costa Rican surrealist whose poetry is forthcoming in *Notre Dame Review*; *Image*; *Bayou Magazine* and has appeared in *32 Poems*; *The Spectacle*; *Welter*; *Verse Daily*; *The Florida Review*; *Green Mountains Review*; *Water~Stone Review'* *DIAGRAM*; *PALABRITAS*; *Forklift, Ohio*; *Hotel Amerika*; *Strange Horizons*; etc. His 2019 debut poetry collection, *Blue Whale Phenomena*, was published by Otis Books (Otis College of Art and Design. Los Angeles, CA).

Anuel Rodriguez (he/him) is a Mexican American poet living in the San Francisco Bay Area. His work has appeared or is forthcoming in *Glass: A Journal of Poetry*, *DREGINALD*, *decomP*, the *Acentos Review*, and elsewhere.

Jess Saldaña's teaching, facilitating, and creative work engage with studies of disability justice, racial capitalism, ecology, and queer aesthetics. They have a longstanding interest in the protean nature of identity, play, perception, and environment. They currently work as the Visual & Multimedia Resources manager at Pratt Institute

Libraries and are a psychoanalytic candidate at the Harlem Family Institute focusing on intersubjective play in trans and mixed race children and adults. Their essay *The Analytic Goodbye: Memory, Primary Narcissism and Dreams* was declared the winner of the 2024 Society for Psychoanalysis and Psychoanalytic Psychology Division 39 Candidate Essay Contest. Writing, photographs, paintings, and drawings have been featured in the following; *Stonewall's Legacy: Poetry Anthology* (2019), *Entropy Magazine* (2019), *Hyperallergic* (2020), *LAMBDA Lit* (2023), *Sinister Wisdom* (2023), *The Brooklyn Rail* (2024), among others. They have presented scholarly work as a part of Black Portraiture[s] 2019 alongside Angela Davis, poetry for The New Museum's education programming, and have composed music for the 2021 promotional trailer for Visual AIDS' Day With(out) Art: ENDURING CARE. In 2021 they were a NYFA City Artist Corps Grant recipient and were awarded Jane Goodall's Roots and Shoots grant.

David M. de León (he/him) is a Puerto Rican writer, academic, and theater artist from New Jersey. He has a Ph.D. from Yale University and served as a senior editor at the *Yale Review*.

David's poetry manuscript *The Cats of Old San Juan* was a finalist for the PANK Book Prize and for the Letras Latinas Andrés Montoya Poetry Prize. His previous manuscript, *On a Field in the Present*, was shortlisted for the Dorset Prize at Tupelo and the Lena-Miles Wever Todd Prize at Pleiades. He was a Tin House Summer Scholar and a scholarship recipient at the Fine Arts Work Center. His work is included in Best of the Net 2021.

His poetry appears or is forthcoming in places like *AGNI*, *Fence Magazine*, *[PANK]*, *DIAGRAM*, the *Indiana Review*, the *Volta*, *Up the Staircase Quarterly*, *Acentos Review*, *Pleiades*, *At Length*, *Strange Horizons*, *Bat City Review*, *2River View*, *Anderbo*, the *Cortland Review*, *Anti-*, the *Adirondack Review*, and the anthologies *Até Mais: Latinx Futurisms* and *Only The Sea Keeps*.

Luis Lopez-Maldonado is a Xicanx activist, poeta, playwright, dancer, choreographer, and educator born and raised in multiple barrios across el Orange County, CA. He/Him/They/Them have two forthcoming books, titled *Gay Poetics of the Passion*, from FlowerSong Press (2024), and *Mexican Bird*, from Querencia Press (2024). They earned a Bachelor of Arts degree from the University of California Riverside, in Creative Writing and Dance. His/Their poetry has been seen in *The American Poetry Review*, *Foglifter*, *Public Pool*, and *Latina Outsiders: Remaking Latina Identity*, among many others. He/They also earned a Master of Arts degree in Dance from Florida State University and a Master of Fine Arts degree in Creative Writing from the University of Notre Dame. He/They are currently adding glitter to the Land of Enchantment, working for the public educational system as a high school Bilingual Educator and Special Education Teacher, holding a Pre K-12 Special Education License and a Pre K-12 Specialty Area License, with endorsements in TESOL, Bilingual Education, Performing Arts, and English Language Arts. He/They are currently a graduate student at the University of New Mexico, to become a principal.

Gustavo Hernandez is the author of the poetry collection *Flower Grand First* (Moon Tide Press). He holds a degree in creative writing from California State University Long Beach and is a poetry editor for the *Cortland Review*. His poems have been published in *Reed, Acentos Review, Sonora Review,* and other publications. He was born in Jalisco, Mexico, and lives in Southern California.

Roda Avelar (she/they) is a trans woman poet from Fresno, California. She earned an MFA in creative writing from the University of California Riverside, where she taught creative writing and English composition, and a BA in English literature from California State University Fresno. She was a Milkweed Editions summer intern in 2019. Avelar is the winner of a 2023 Ruth Lilly and Dorothy Sargent Rosenberg Fellowship and was a 2022 Community of Writers fellow. Her poetry can be found in *The Acentos Review, SPORAZINE, ANMLY, About Place Journal, Poetry Magazine, Pleiades,* and *Flies, Cockroaches & Poets*. She creates work that imagines queer people and people of color in science fiction, mythology, and queer liberation.

Steven Alvarez is the author of *The Codex Mojaodicus,* winner of the Fence Modern Poets Prize. He has also authored the novels in verse Manhatitlán, published by The Operating System, and *McTlán,* published by FlowerSong Press. His work has appeared in the *Best Experimental Writing* (BAX), *Berkeley Poetry Review, Fence, Huizache,* the *Offing,* and *Waxwing*. Follow Steven on Instagram @stevenpaulalvarez and Twitter @chastitellez.

C.T. Salazar is a Latinx poet and librarian from Mississippi. He's the author of *Headless John the Baptist Hitchhiking,* out now from Acre Books, and three previous chapbooks. He's the 2020 recipient of the Mississippi Institute of Arts and Letters Award in poetry. His poems have most recently appeared in *West Branch, Cincinnati Review, Gulf Coast, Denver Quarterly, Hopkins Review, Southeast Review, Beloit Poetry Journal, Pleiades,* and elsewhere.

Sara Borjas is a self-identified Xicanx pocha and a Fresno poet. Her debut collection, *Heart Like a Window, Mouth Like a Cliff* (Noemi Press, 2019), received a 2020 American Book Award. Sara was featured as one of Poets & Writers 2019 Debut Poets. She has received fellowships from MacDowell, CantoMundo, Postgraduate Writers Conference, and Community of Writers. She believes that all Black lives matter and will resist white supremacy until Black liberation is realized. She teaches creative writing at CSU East Bay but stays rooted in Fresno.

Influenced by a childhood spent between Oregon and Guatemala, the art and writing of **Stephanie Adams-Santos** delve into the ancestral, primal, and mythological forces that shape inner life. They are the author of several full-length poetry collections and chapbooks, including *Dream of Xibalba* (selected by Jericho Brown as winner of the 2021 Orison Poetry Prize; finalist for a 2024 Oregon Book Award and Lambda Literary Award) and *Swarm Queen's Crown* (finalist for a 2016 Lambda Literary Award). In addition to their literary work, Stephanie writes for television, radio, and film.

Roberto Carlos Garcia writes poetry and prose about the Afro-Latinx and Afro-Diasporic experience. His work has been published widely in places like *Poetry Magazine, NACLA, Poets & Writers, The Root,* and others. Garcia is a 2023 New Jersey State Council of the Arts Poetry Fellow and the author of five books. Four poetry collections: *Melancolía, black / Maybe: An Afro Lyric, [Elegies], What Can I Tell You: Selected Poems,* and one essay collection, *Traveling Freely,* forthcoming in autumn 2024 from Curbstone Books / Northwestern University Press. Garcia is the founder of Get Fresh Books Publishing, a literary nonprofit.

Raina J. León, PhD, is Black, Afro-Boricua, and from Philadelphia (Lenni Lenape ancestral lands). She is a mother, daughter, sister, madrina, comadre, partner, poet, writer, and teacher educator. She believes in collective action and community work, the profound power of holding space for the telling of our stories, and the liberatory practice of humanizing education. She seeks out communities of care and craft and is a member of the Carolina African American Writers Collective, Cave Canem, CantoMundo, Macondo and Obsidian Foundation, among others. She is the author of *black god mother this body, Canticle of Idols, Boogeyman Dawn, sombra : (dis) locate,* and the chapbooks *profeta without refuge* and *Areyto to Atabey: Essays on the Mother(ing) Self.* She publishes across forms in visual art, poetry, nonfiction, fiction, and scholarly work. She is a founding editor of *The Acentos Review*, an online, quarterly, international journal devoted to the promotion and publication of Latinx arts, which has published over one thousand Latinx voices since 2008. She recently retired early as a full professor of education at Saint Mary's College of California, only the third Black person (all Black women) and the first Afro-Latina to achieve that rank there. She currently supports poets and writers at the Stonecoast MFA at the University of Southern Maine. She is additionally a frequent guest speaker, emerging visual artist, writing coach, curriculum developer, and podcaster with Generational Archives and a digital archivist with StoryJoy, which she co-founded with her mother, Dr. Norma Thomas. You can find her on all the platforms @rainaleon.

Monique Quintana is a Xicana from Fresno, CA, and the author of *Cenote City* (Clash Books, 2019) and the chapbook *My Favorite Sancho and Other Fairy Tales* (Sword and Kettle Press, 2021). Her work has appeared in *Pank, Wildness, Winter Tangerine,* the *Acentos Review,* and other publications. You can find her book reviews and artist interviews at *Luna Luna Magazine,* where she is a contributing editor. Her writing has been supported by Yaddo, the Sundress Academy of the Arts, the Community of Writers, and the Kimmel Harding Nelson Center. You can find her on Twitter at @ quintanadarkling and moniquequintana.com.

Adriana M. Martínez Figueroa (they/she) is a bisexual Puerto Rican writer, editor, and sensitivity reader. They hold a B.A. from Iowa State University in Women and Gender Studies with a minor in US Latinx Studies. Their words can be found on *Bustle, Tor.com, Boricua en la Luna* (2019), and *Good For Her: An Anthology of Women's Wrongs* (2024). They live in Vega Baja, PR with their family and three beautiful cats. Follow them on social media @boricuareads and check out their website boricuareads.com.

From where willow trees grow wild on Detroit's Eastside; Conant Gardens raised **Franchesca Lamarre**. She is a private art school dropout; Pratt & CCS. Her photo and curatorial works are featured in Contemporary And (C&), Fader, Münchner Kammerspiele, NY Times, and Detroit's *MetroTimes.* She has traveled throughout the United States teaching BlackFuturist frameworks at the intersections of art, tech, and social justice. She is co-founder of internationally attended #AfroFutureFEST, most known for its ticket prices, Black Detroit music, and Black youth.

She is the director of *VIRAGO,* an experimental arts documentary following the stylization and presence of five Detroit Black & Femme identifying music artist. Through a queedome archetype she demands for the reimagining of autonomy in Black, femme, and Queer media. She is a Detroit Black-Futurist hoping to evoke active introspection and presence within worlds unimagined by the Black eye. Presently, she is the creator and host of @WeGon'GetFREE! (a podcast, visual dialogue, and archiving label). Lamarre co-authors strategies towards freedom with co-hosts and listeners weekly.

Franchesca is currently researching how the intersections of tech, art, and speculative play can conjure up more just and exciting worlds for BlPOC and Queer folks. Franchesca spends her down time indulging in lavender baths, being still with nature, cooking, making mixes, and organizing co-dreaming spaces for readers (#COMPLEXpeople), coders (#CODEKINK), and critical thinkers (#CriticalConversations) alike! Franchesca has lived with the deep gut intuition that her role in this world is the challenger; asking all of us to diverge from nomenclatures that reduce our robust lived experiences. She is in search of the rememory of everybody free.

Bailey Cohen (he/him) is the Assistant Editor for Borderlands: Texas Poetry Review. A poet, essayist, and book reviewer, his work has appeared or is forthcoming in publications such as *Shenandoah, The Iowa Review, Poet Lore, Waxwing, The Spectacle, Poetry Northwest,* and *Sugar House Review*, among others. He has received numerous Best of the Net and Pushcart Prize nominations, and his work has been featured in several anthologies such as *The BreakBeat Poets Vol.4: LatiNEXT*. Serving as the organizer of the Strange Tools Writer's Workshop, Bailey is a Wiley Birkhofer Fellow in Poetry at NYU. He is researching and writing about labor movements and U.S. interventions in Latin America, magical realism, postcolonial theory, and more.

Leila Ortiz (she/her) is of Puerto Rican, Cuban, and Irish descent, born and raised in New York City. She is the author of two chapbooks, *Girl Life* (Recreation League 2016) and *A Mouth Is Not a Place* (Dancing Girl Press 2017). Leila's poems have appeared in *ANMLY, Apogee, Sixth Finch, Tinderbox,* and the *Recluse,* among other publications. Her work was anthologized in *The Best Microfiction 2020* and *The Familiar Wild: On Dogs & Poetry*. She was a featured poet on *The Slowdown Podcast* with Tracy K. Smith. Leila lives in Brooklyn with her dog Sirius Black.

Victoria Mallorga Hernandez is a queer Peruvian poet and editor. She is a graduate of the Emerson College Publishing and Writing MA and a literary agent associate at Writers House. She has been a reader for *POETRY* magazine and associate poetry editor of *Redivider* and *Verboser*. Victoria's poems have appeared in *Thin Air, Cream City Review, Círculo de poesía, La primera vértebra, Revista Lucerna, Plástico,* and anthologies throughout South America, Spain, and the U.S. She is the author of the books *albión* (Alastor Editores, 2019) and *Dos chicas al borde de la cama* (Valparaíso

Ediciones, 2024) as well as an illustrated chapbook, *absolución* (2020). Find her as @ cielosraros or in victoria-mallorga.carrd.co. She lived in Brooklyn, New York.

Leslie Sainz is the author of *Have You Been Long Enough at Table* (Tin House, 2023), a finalist for the 2024 Audre Lorde Award. The daughter of Cuban exiles, her work has appeared in the Academy of American Poets' *Poem-a-Day*, the *Yale Review*, *Kenyon Review*, *American Poetry Review*, and elsewhere. A three-time National Poetry Series finalist, she's received fellowships from the National Endowment for the Arts, CantoMundo, and the Stadler Center for Poetry & Literary Arts at Bucknell University. Originally from Miami, she lives in Vermont and works as the managing editor of *New England Review*.

P. L. Sanchez (he/him) is an ESL teacher from Lima, Peru. His work has appeared in *jubilat*, *Fifth Wednesday Journal*, and *Bayou*, among others.

Jose Hernandez Diaz is a 2017 NEA Poetry Fellow. He is the author of *The Fire Eater* (Texas Review Press, 2020). His work appears in the *American Poetry Review*, *Boulevard*, *Colorado Review*, *Georgia Review*, *Iowa Review*, the *Missouri Review*, *Poetry*, the *Southern Review*, the *Yale Review*, and in *The Best American Nonrequired Reading Anthology 2011*. He teaches creative writing online and edits for Frontier Poetry.

Alessandra Nysether-Santos is a Brazilian American writer and educator living in Florida. She was a finalist for the 2023 James Applewhite Poetry Competition, and you can find her writing in places like *NCLR*, *Sad Girl Review*, *SOUP CAN Magazine*, and the *lickety-split*. Their poem "fat woman utopia!" was featured on the Space538 2021 Poetry Hotline. They're on Twitter @poetalessandra

Michelle Moncayo is a Dominican/Ecuadorian poet in New Jersey. She received a 2020 Fellowship from the New Jersey State Council on the Arts. Her work explores diaspora, queer identity, and mental/physical illness. She has received fellowships from SPACE at Ryder Farm, Vermont Studio Center, Sundress Academy for the Arts, CantoMundo, and VONA. Her poetry has appeared or is forthcoming in *Até Mais: Latinx Futurisms*, *Broadsided Press*, *No Tender Fences: An Anthology of Immigrant & First-Generation American Poetry*, *Palette Poetry*, and *Ninth Letter*. You can find more of her work at michellemoncayoart.net & on Instagram @mmon1392.